PLANNING PERMISSION

THE ESSENTIAL
GUIDE FOR
HOMEOWNERS

Kenneth A. Dijksman,
BA(Hons) DipTP, MRTPI

COURTLAND
❖❖❖
B O O K S

Published by:

Courtland Books,
60 Berkeley Road,
Newbury,
Berkshire.
RG14 5JG

© K.A. Dijksman 1992

Whilst every care has been taken in the preparation of the information contained
in this book, no liability can be accepted for any loss or damage arising either
directly or indirectly out of reliance on this book or any part of it.

The advice contained in this book is provided as an addition to, rather than as a
substitute for, the advice of your Local Planning Authority.

Illustrated by Kim Jagoe with the kind assistance of Ian Douglas.

Model Application reproduced courtesy of Michael F. Wilson-Doyle M.I.Arch.S.
Tel: (0491) 671285

PREFACE

If you are considering building an extension, a conservatory, a new garage, a workshop, a new wall or fence, or any other major home improvement, planning permission may be required, but sometimes it isn't, it may be granted or it may not, different rules apply to different areas, even to different houses, it all depends ...

Without the right information, seeking to obtain planning permission (or finding out whether it is needed) can be confusing, frustrating and expensive. Yet the vast majority of people seem to be unaware of how the planning system works and any advice you do receive may simply reflect the priorities of those who give it.

In many cases the grant of planning permission will mean the difference between continuing to enjoy an existing home or having to move somewhere else to find additional space. Even if what is applied for is not built the grant of permission alone can make a property more attractive to potential buyers.

This book has been written as a straight forward laymans guide to planning, to give homeowners a better understanding of what they are likely to be allowed to do to their property and to help them avoid unnecessary problems.

Chapter 1 acts as an easy reference to the rest of the book and answers a range of basic questions which should be asked by anyone contemplating making major changes to their home.

Chapters 2 to 8 give information and practical advice on all those aspects of the planning system which are likely to be encountered. This includes Tree Preservation Orders, How to Object to Someone Else's Planning Application, Appealing Against a Refusal, Obtaining Building Regulations Approval, and How Planning Controls are Enforced and more.

Chapter 9 is a brief introduction to the system of Building Regulations which will be relevant in most cases.

This guide will help you in deciding what the possibilities are for improving your own property and it will enable you to approach the problem of obtaining planning permission with confidence.

N.B. The advice given in this guide does **not** relate to Listed Buildings.

———— ◆ ————

CONTENTS

Chapter 1
The Basic Questions

	Page No.
What is planning permission?	1
What does planning permission control?	1
What does planning permission not control?	1
Is planning permission always required?	1
To whom do you apply?	2
Who makes the decision?	2
How long does planning permission last?	2
What happens to an application?	3
What criteria will be used to judge a proposal?	3
What service will be available?	4
Can you draw the plans yourself?	4
Who do you employ to design your proposal and draw the plans?	5
Should you use a professional agent?	5
What happens if somebody objects to a proposal?	6
Can you appeal against a refusal?	6
Can you change a proposal once it has received planning permission?	6
Is planning about conformity?	7

Chapter 2
Permitted Development

Designated areas	8
Planning conditions	8
Article 4 Directions	9
Other considerations	9
Useful definitions	9
Permitted development rights explained	11
Extensions	11
Roof extensions	11
Roof lights/sky lights	12
Solar panels	12
Outbuildings and enclosures	12
Domestic heating oil storage tanks	14
Porches	14
Fences, walls and gates	14
Accesses	15
Driveways, hardstandings and patios	15
Parking	15
Integral garages	16
Swimming pools, ponds	16
Satellite dishes	16
Working from home	17
Granny annexes	18

CONTENTS (Continued)

Share houses   19
Maintenance and repairs   19
Demolition and rebuilding   19
Written confirmation   20
Certificates of lawful use or development   20

Chapter 3
Submitting a Planning Application

The procedure   22
How long does it take?   23
Before you submit the application   23
Submitting the application   24
The role of Councillors   24
Types of application   25
The planning application itself   26
The fee   26
The application forms   26
The ownership certificate   28
The plans   29
Existing plans   29
The application site   30
What sort of decision can be made?   30
Conditions   30
Making an application on land you do not own   31
Applications affecting boundaries   31
Land ownership   32
Planning application checklist   32

Chapter 4
What will get Planning Permission?

Planning - an art not a science   33
A major investment   33
General principles   34
Areas which have special designations   34
Other considerations   35
The basic principles   36
Front extensions   41
Side extensions   43
Rear extensions   48
Roof conversions   52
Extensions to houses in open countryside   56
Outbuildings and garages   56
Materials and attention to detail   57
Parking and access   60
Hard surfacing   61
Design checklist   62
A house in your garden?   63
Building plot examples   65

Chapter 5
Appealing Against Refusal

Reasons for refusal   67
What can be appealed against?   68
Should you appeal?   68
Cost and time   69
Who decides the outcome of a planning appeal?   69
What sort of appeal should you make?   69
Which sort of appeal is best?   71
Who can appeal?   71
What do you say?   71
Will the Planning Department help you to appeal?   74
What if you lose the appeal?   74
'Unreasonable' decisions   74
The Ombudsman   75

Chapter 6
How to object to someone else's Planning Application

Why bother?   76
Finding out about the application   76
How do you object?   76
What do you say?   77
How do you say it?   78

Chapter 7
How Unauthorised Development is Controlled

Enforcement   80
Safe after four years   80
Will enforcement action always be taken?   81
Negotiation and request for retrospective application   81
Requests for further information   81
Enforcement notice   82
Appealing against the enforcement notice   82
Stop notices   82
Time   83
Enforcement of conditions   83
Amended plans   83

Chapter 8
Trees

Tree Preservation Orders   85
Trees in Conservation Areas   86
Planning conditions   86
Trees and your planning application   86

Chapter 9
Building Consent and Regulations

Is building regulation approval required?   **88**
Making a building regulations application   **89**
Building regulation fees   **91**
Do neighbours have the right to object?   **91**
Can you appeal?   **91**
What happens if your work does not comply?   **92**
Are there penalties for contravening building regulations?   **92**
Information on building standards   **92**

Appendix

Model Applications

Glossary of Terms

Chapter 1

THE BASIC QUESTIONS

Chapter 1
THE BASIC QUESTIONS

What is Planning Permission?

Planning permission is necessary because various Town and Country Planning Acts of Parliament require Local Authorities to control what can be built, and how buildings and land are used. Planning permission is applied for by using particular forms and plans (see page 26) and it is granted or refused, in writing, (see page 30) by the Local Planning Authority.

———— ◆ ————

What does Planning Permission Control?

Planning permission is concerned with:

*   the location, appearance and use of proposed new buildings
*   changes in the appearance and size of existing buildings
*   changes in the use of existing buildings or land.

———— ◆ ————

What does Planning Permission Not Control?

*   Planning permission does not concern itself with how a building is built. A separate system of building regulations is involved (see page 88).

*   Nor does it effect property ownership or other legal interests or covenants relating to property.

*   Planning permission is not (except in very unusual circumstances) the property of an individual. It relates to the land itself, regardless of who currently or in the future may own it, or who actually made the planning application (see page 31).

———— ◆ ————

Is Planning Permission always required?

No. In relation to private houses, there are a range of alterations and structures which may be built onto a house or garden which do not require planning permission. Such development is known as permitted development (explained further in Chapter 2).

———— ◆ ————

To whom do you apply?

England and Wales

The relevant Planning Departments are currently found in:

* District Councils
* Borough Councils
* City Councils
* National Park Authorities.

These Local Authorities are the Local Planning Authority for their area.

Scotland

* District Authorities
* Highland Regional Councils
* City Councils

Who Makes the Decision?

Planning applications are determined either by a Planning Committee made up of elected Councillors or by the most senior planner, the Chief Planning Officer (see page 24). A decision made by the Chief Planning Officer is known as a decision made under delegated authority.

If an application is put before committee there will usually be a recommendation made by a Planning Officer as to how it should be determined.

Small scale proposals (such as house extensions or single new houses) will often not be put before a committee unless there has been an objection from a neighbour, the Parish Council, Town Council, or any other member of the public.

Planning Committee meetings are open to the public but only a limited number of Planning Authorities allow either objectors or applicants to speak at them.

How Long does Planning Permission last?

Planning permission usually lasts for 5 years, in some circumstances this may be reduced (see page 26).

What Happens to an Application?

When an application is submitted:

*   It will first be checked to see if it is complete and, if it is, it will be registered.

*   Consultations will be carried out with public bodies such as the highway authority and local Parish or Town Councils.

*   Publicity will be given to allow neighbours the opportunity to comment.

*   Your house will be visited by a Planning Officer. You may be aksed to submit more information or to amend your application.

*   The application will be considered by the Planning Committee or by the Chief Planning Officer.

*   Shortly after the application has been determined, you will receive a decision notice.

A more comprehensive description of this procedure is given in Chapter 3.

What Criteria will be used to Judge a Proposal?

Applications for extensions and other domestic proposals will usually be judged on the basis of:

*   The Planning Authority's own planning policies and government policy.

*   The history of planning decisions related to the property in question and its neighbourhood.

*   The effect of what is proposed upon the residential environment of neighbouring houses.

*   The suitability of the design and appearance of the extension relative to the character of the house and its surroundings.

*   Whether the extension will affect the amount of parking spaces required or available, or affect highway safety.

Further advice is given in Chapter 4.

What Service will be available?

Planning Departments are usually open office hours Monday to Friday.

Current and past planning applications will be available for you to inspect, usually by appointment.

Professional Planning Officers will be available to answer your enquiries and to advise you (see Chapter 5) by phone, at the planning office and possibly out of the office on site. All departments have their own systems, appointments are sometimes necessary.

Many Planning Departments produce guidance documents and leaflets available free to the public to assist them in making applications.

The necessary planning and building regulations application forms will be available, and can either be collected at the Council Offices or they will be sent to you.

When dealing with Planning Officers, be friendly, be polite, don't be afraid to ask questions (see Chapter 5). The local Councillors are your elected representatives and they can be approached quite legitimately by both applicants or objectors who wish to promote their own point of view.

Although the legal responsibilities of all Planning Departments are the same, the quality of service to the public, and the speed of service given can vary enormously throughout the country.

———————— ◆ ————————

Can you Draw the Plans Yourself?

Most people do not have the knowledge or ability to draw the plans required to make a planning application (see page 26). The plans required to make a building regulations application (see Chapter 9) are even more difficult to produce. As a result having plans professionally drawn is usually adviseable.

When building regulations are not required (e.g. for a conservatory) or the development is very small and is to be dealt with using the card notification system of building control then drawing the plans yourself may be possible. Having a copy of the original plans for your house (see page 29) could make it a fairly simple exercise if you can draw accurately with a scale rule.

When making an application for a conservatory it may be possible to get away with a location plan, site plan and photographs of the house and copies of the manufacturer's literature. Some authorities will accept this so it could be worth a try. If they don't, you have only lost some time.

———————— ◆ ————————

Who do you Employ to Design your Proposal and Draw the Plans?

There are many people who design extensions etc. and draw plans for planning applications. They include professional architects, architectural technicians, builders, surveyors and many others.

The ability and experience of the person you choose will have a direct bearing on the quality of the building created and value for money which is obtained.

It is important that the person you employ should demonstrate:

* a successful track record;
* examples of previous work, now built;
* an interest in good quality design;
* a willingness and desire to understand what you want out of the proposal;
* a serious commitment to value for money, not just cheap prices.

It is also important that you feel very comfortable dealing with them.

A reasonable way to find someone to design and draw up your proposal is to ask another homeowner whose extension you like, or to ask an established local builder. A personal recommendation from a friend is usually the best way.

When establishing the cost of the project ensure that you understand clearly what service the fee includes, such as all revised plans necessary to obtain Planning and Building Regulation approval. The invitation and evaluation of tenders (you should insist upon a minimum of three tenders), overseeing the work during the contract period etc.

————————— ◆ —————————

Should you use a Professional Agent?

It is likely that whoever designs your proposal and draws the plans required for the planning application will also offer to act as your agent. As such they will submit the application and carry out the pre-application discussions and subsequent negotiations with the Planning Department.

Whether you decide to utilise the services of an agent is clearly a matter of individual choice and will depend to some extent upon how confident you feel at the prospect of dealing with officialdom. Employing an agent should not prevent you from getting involved at any stage if you want to.

A professional agent is likely to have:

* a broad knowledge of planning;
* experience in negotiating with the Planners;
* the ability to arrive at architectural solutions to problems.

A professional agent can be useful in defusing the potential for neighbour disputes and other personal conflicts by acting as an independent third party who is not emotionally involved in any particular proposal.

–––––––––– ◆ ––––––––––

What Happens if somebody objects to a Proposal?

Just because someone objects does not mean that a planning application will necessarily be refused, and just because no-one objects does not mean that permission will be granted. It is quite possible that a neighbour or the Parish or Town Council may not like what you wish to do, regardless of its acceptability in planning terms.

Many objections to planning applications by neighbours etc are based on envy, personal dislike, fear of property devaluation or ignorance of what is proposed. Some objections, such as concern about overlooking windows, overshadowing or loss of sunlight to windows, or concern about noise and disturbance from commercial activity etc, may be well founded. It is the job of Planning Officers to distinguish between the two. The consequence of an objection is that the application will usually need to go before the Planning Committee for determination. The danger is that the committee may refuse an application because of sympathy for the objector rather than because the application is genuinely harmful. (See Chapter 6).

Before submitting a planning application you are advised to talk to your neighbour about it to explain what you intend.

–––––––––– ◆ ––––––––––

Can you Appeal against a Refusal?

Yes, but it could take up to six months and a minimum of four before you receive a decision from the Planning Inspectorate at the Department of the Environment. There is no fee charged by the DOE and in some cases it could be the best way of achieving what you want. In many cases it should be possible to negotiate an approval for the extension, garage or whatever you wish to build by reducing the size, changing the location or making changes to its appearance. Whether you appeal depends on how strongly you are committed to your original idea of what you want and what sort of chance you may have of succeeding. (See Chapter 5).

–––––––––– ◆ ––––––––––

Can you Change a Proposal once it has received Planning Permission?

Yes, most Planning Authorities will accept minor amendments to the approved plans provided that such changes do not significantly affect the nature of the proposal or cause harm. (See page 83).

–––––––––– ◆ ––––––––––

Is Planning about Conformity?

This is not a book about architecture. The advice given in Chapter 4 is not intended to preach universal conformity in how people improve their homes or design their extensions etc. There is considerable freedom for individuality in the design of houses in normal residential areas.

Unless a Planning Authority identify specific characteristics of an area as being visually important, then just because something is different from its neighbours does not mean that it will be refused. You should not be afraid to be original and incorporate interesting and imaginative elements into the appearance of your home. In a recent appeal decision which permitted a fibre glass shark in the roof of a house in Headington, Oxford, the Inspector stated that it was <u>not</u> the purpose of planning to enforce a "boring and mediocre uniformity" on the built environment.

◆

Chapter 2

PERMITTED DEVELOPMENT

Chapter 2
PERMITTED DEVELOPMENT

Permitted development is a term used to describe things which a homeowner can construct without the need to make a planning application. This is a potentially confusing subject, but if it is approached methodically it will become clear that a lot can be done without the need to obtain planning permission.

Permitted development rights apply to the majority of <u>houses</u> and they are, in effect, a general permission granted by central government for a wide range of minor works. These rights do not apply to <u>flats</u> other than with regard to the erection of a limited number of Satellite Dishes (see page 16).

Permitted Development rights are not the same countrywide and are occasionally modified by Local Planning Authorities. Therefore in the first instance it is useful to establish whether your house still has the benefit of the full range of these rights. The following factors need to be considered:

———— ◆ ————

Designated Areas

What is allowed as permitted development is more restricted within the areas of:

* National Parks
* Areas of Outstanding Natural Beauty
* Conservation Areas
* The Norfolk and Suffolk Broads.

———— ◆ ————

Planning Conditions

In some situations, typically on high density housing estates, the planning permission granted for the houses will contain a condition removing all or some of the permitted development rights. For instance, on some estates the right to enclose front gardens by 1m high fences is removed, so that the estates remain open plan. Where houses have integral garages the right to convert these garages into rooms is sometimes removed, to ensure that future parking provision is adequate.

———— ◆ ————

Article 4 Directions

A Local Authority can remove or reduce Permitted Development Rights by serving an Article 4 Direction. This will remain in force for six months during which it must be confirmed by the Department of the Environment. Once confirmed it is then permanent. The Local Authority must give justification for this Direction and anyone whose property is affected can appeal to the Department of the Environment. If planning permission is refused for a development which would have been Permitted Development had it not been for an Article 4 Direction then compensation may be payable for the loss in property value incurred.

◆

Other Considerations

Legal covenants

Irrespective of whether planning permission is required or is granted, some properties have had restrictions placed on their deeds by previous owners or the original builder. For instance, builders sometimes remove the right to enclose front gardens or the right to park a caravan in the garden, in order to maintain a certain appearance in an estate. Removing these restrictive covenants, where they exist, is a legal matter between the property owner and the owner of the covenant.

Previous extensions

Permitted development rights do enable houses to be extended a certain amount before planning permission is required. Once the maximum has been reached all further additions require permission. This means that if your house has been extended in the past, your right to extend may have been partially or entirely used up. If an extension is so large that it exceeds the maximum allowed as permitted development and it is granted planning permission and built, all further extensions will require permission.

◆

Useful Definitions

Before explaining the details of what may be done without permission a small number of phrases are explained. These phrases will not make much sense until you attempt to understand how the permitted development regulations relate to your own property. Further definitions of planning jargon are given in the glossary.

* **The original house**

  The phrase 'original house' is used in the rules to refer to the house as it was first built, prior to any additions. If a house was built prior to 1st July 1948, the definition of 'original house' is as the house stood on that date.

* Extensions

(1) This does include conservatories. In permitted development terms, a conservatory is treated as an extension.

(2) Any outbuildings built in your garden since the house, which are located within 5m of any part of the house, will count against the permitted development allowance for extensions. So in effect they are treated as an extension.

(3) Any extension to the original house which would come within 5m of any existing outbuilding will cause that outbuilding to be treated as an extension in terms of the permitted development allowance.

(4) Where outbuildings (including garages) were built at the same time as the original house and closer to it than 5m, these outbuildings will be considered as if they were part of the original house for the purposes of calculating the amount of permitted development available.

(5) In those areas mentioned in Designated Areas on page 8, all outbuildings which are more than 10 cubic metres in size and which were built after the original house are treated as if they are extensions to the house and count against the permitted development allowance.

* Volume

Measurements of volume are used extensively in describing the amount which can be built as permitted development. All such measurements are based on external dimensions, and it includes the roof.

* Height

Where measurements of height are used in relation to buildings it is assumed that the measurement is taken from ground level immediately adjacent to the building which is being erected. If the levels vary, the measurement is taken from the highest part of the ground. In the case of walls and fences if ground levels vary then the measurement is taken from the surrounding 'natural' ground level.

* Highway

When used in relation to walls and fences this only refers to roads which carry vehicular traffic, but it includes the width of the footpath or verges on either side. So when distances are measured from 'the highway' they will usually be taken from the property boundary next to the road. When used in relation to distances from the house itself or extensions to the house, the term 'highway' includes footpaths, not just roads which carry vehicles. In both cases, the term refers to any highway which runs along any boundary of the house, not just at the front.

———————— ♦ ————————

Permitted development rights explained

Extensions

You will not require planning permission to extend your house provided that you comply with the following.

* **Position**

    No extension should be built closer to any highway than any part of the existing house, unless the distance between the extension and the highway is 20m or more. No more than half of the area of land around the original house should be covered by extensions (or other additional buildings).

* **Size**

    In the case of a terraced (or end terrace) house or within the areas mentioned in Designated Areas on page 8, the maximum size of extension is 10% of the volume of the original house or up to 50 cubic metres, whichever is the greater. For other kinds of houses including bungalows, outside those areas mentioned in Designated Areas on page 8, the maximum allowed is 15% of the volume of the original house or up to 70 cubic metres, whichever is the greater. In any case the maximum should not exceed a total of 115 cubic metres.

* **Height**

    If the extension is within 2m of the boundary of the property it must not exceed 4m in height. If the extension is 2m or more from the boundary the extension must not be higher than the highest part of the roof of the original house.

————————— ◆ —————————

Roof Extensions

This refers to extensions and alterations to the roof of the original house, and includes dormer windows. Planning permission is required for any additions or extensions to the roof of a house if it is located within any of the areas mentioned in Designated Areas on page 8. Outside those areas, you will not require planning permission provided that you comply with the following:

* **Position**

    No additions or extensions are allowed on any roof slope which faces a highway.

* **Size**

    The maximum size which may be added to the roof of a terraced (or end terrace) house is 40 cubic metres.

For other kinds of houses, including bungalows, the maximum permitted is 50 cubic metres.

These quantities are permitted as part of, and not in addition to, the maximum amounts available for extensions.

* **Height**

No roof extension should be higher than the highest part of the original house. (Excluding chimneys).

———————— ◆ ————————

Roof Lights/Sky Lights

Planning permission is not required for roof lights, on any roof slope.

———————— ◆ ————————

Solar Panels

The installation of solar panels is acceptable provided that they do not project significantly beyond the roof slope.

———————— ◆ ————————

Outbuildings and Enclosures

This includes garages, car ports, sheds, workshops, greenhouses, tennis court fences, summer houses and swimming pool enclosures - in fact any outbuilding or structure which is built for your private enjoyment. An unlimited number of such buildings can be built on your land without the need to obtain planning permission provided that you comply with the following:

* **Position**

No outbuilding should be built closer to any highway than any part of the existing house, unless the distance between the outbuilding and the highway is 20m or more.

No more than half of the area of land around the original house should be covered by such outbuildings (or extensions).

Outbuildings positioned within 5 metres of the house will be considered as extensions for the purposes of permitted development (see definitions on page 10).

* **Size**

Within those areas described in Designated Areas on page 8, any outbuilding of more than 10 cubic metres in size, anywhere in the garden of the house, will require planning permission and will also count as an extension and be deducted from the permitted development allowance for extensions.

Outside those areas there are no restrictions on the actual size of the outbuildings constructed, other than in terms of height and position.

* **Height**

Buildings or structures should not be more than 3m in height, or 4m if the building has a ridged (ie pitched) roof.

* **Use of outbuildings for residential purposes**

Outbuildings may be used to provide living accommodation (for sleeping, eating, washing etc) provided that:

(1) the outbuilding is not used as a separate dwelling;

(2) the outbuilding is used only as an annexe to the main house by a member of the household;

(3) the use of the outbuilding is tied up with, and closely related to, the use of the main house as a private dwelling.

This means, for instance, that whilst the accommodation of an elderly dependent relative in an detached annexe might be acceptable, the use of the outbuilding to provide a cheap home for grown up children would not. It is particularly important that written confirmation is obtained from your local Planning Department that your use of an outbuilding in the manner described in 1, 2 and 3 is acceptable to them. If you encounter difficulty it may be useful to draw to their attention the case of Uttlesford District Council -v- Secretary of State for the Environment and White, March 1991, which is found in the Journal of Planning Law 1992.

* **Think ahead**

Be careful not to construct outbuildings where they would prevent future permitted development extensions. Remember that if an extension comes closer than 5m to an existing outbuilding, that outbuilding would count, itself, as an extension in terms of the permitted development allowance.

Domestic Heating Oil Storage Tanks

These should not exceed 3500 litres in capacity, be more than 3m above ground level and not come between the house and the road as with other structures in the garden. Liquified petroleum gas tanks will always require permission.

———————— ◆ ————————

Porches

You may put a porch on any of the doors to your house provided that:

* **Position**

  It is at least 2m away from the highway.

* **Size**

  It does not exceed $3m^2$ in ground floor area, measured externally.

* **Height**

  It does not exceed 3m in height.

———————— ◆ ————————

Fences, Walls and Gates

The right to build, repair or reposition a fence or wall does not relate to the type of materials used. Planning permission is not required provided that:

* **Height**

  No fence or wall should exceed 1m in height where it is situated directly adjacent to a highway. Elsewhere the maximum height for fences on the boundary of properties is 2m.

* **Position**

  The phrase 'adjacent to the highway' means 'near to' the edge of the highway. Different Planning Authorities operate different interpretations of what this means. In my view if a fence is further than 2 metres from the highway it is not 'adjacent' to it.

* **Safety**

  If you are erecting or re-positioning a fence be careful to avoid blocking sight lines, causing lack of visibility at road junctions. In such cases the Local Authority can decide that permission is required due to the effect on highway safety. On many estates fences are deliberately set back to provide adequate visibility for cars and this may be controlled by a condition on the planning permission for the development.

* **Trees and hedges**

  Planning permission is not usually required to enclose a garden with trees or hedges provided that a condition does not exist which specifically prevents it.

  Such a condition may exist to prevent the blocking of sight lines at road junctions or in other locations where visibility is important.

* **Within the garden**

  Means of enclosure within the garden are governed by the rules related to outbuildings above, in addition to the rules related to fences. So in effect, fences within a garden may be up to 3m in height provided that less than half the garden area is so enclosed.

———— ◆ ————

Accesses

You do not require planning permission to create an access from the road onto your property providing that the road is not a trunk or classified road and that the access does not obstruct sight lines or cause danger. The access must be associated with other minor works not needing planning permission such as the creation of a hardstanding or garage.

In creating the new access, permission to cross the pavement or verge will be required from the highway authority (usually the County Council or in London, the relevant Borough), who will also stipulate the method of construction of the dropped kerb, pavement crossover etc.

———— ◆ ————

Driveways, Hardstandings and Patios

There are no restrictions on the right to create hard surfaces on all or part of your garden, although such hard surfaces must only be used in connection with the private use of the house, ie not in connection with any commercial activity.

———— ◆ ————

Parking

* **Caravans**

  Planning permission is not required to park a caravan in the front or back garden of a house provided that it is not used as separate living accommodation independent of the house itself.

* **Commercial vehicles**

> If the homeowner uses a commercial vehicle as part of their job and parks it at home, overnight and at weekends (as one would a private car) then planning permission may not be required. However, the use of a private house as the base for operating a commercial vehicle business, like a taxi or van hire business, does require permission.

———— ♦ ————

Integral Garages

Permission is not required to convert an integral or attached garage into a room used as part of the house (unless this is prevented by a condition, see page 30).

———— ♦ ————

Swimming Pools, Ponds

Planning permission is not required to create swimming pools or ponds within the garden provided that they, in combination with all extensions and outbuildings, would not cover more than half the area of land around the original house. Any building over a pool would be considered in the same way as any other outbuilding.

———— ♦ ————

Satellite Dishes

Provided that certain rules are complied with, permission is not required for a satellite dish, although it is important that the dish is sited to minimise its visual impact. This is clearly a matter of opinion, so before installing a dish gain the Planning Authority's agreement in writing that the site you have chosen is the one which does 'minimise its visual impact'.

In all areas:

* only one dish is permitted

* it must not protrude above the highest part of the roof

* if located on a chimney, it must not exceed 45cm in diameter or be above the highest part of the chimney stack.

In the following counties the maximum size of dish permitted is 90cm:

Cleveland, Cornwall, Cumbria, Devon, Durham, Dyfed, Greater Manchester, Gwynedd, Humberside, Lancashire, Merseyside, Northumberland, North Yorkshire, South Yorkshire, Tyne and Wear, West Glamorgan, West Yorkshire.

Outside these counties the maximum size permitted is 70cm. If a house is located in a national park, Area of Outstanding Natural Beauty, Conservation Area or the Norfolk Broads, then in addition to these rules:

* the dish must not be located on a chimney

* the dish must not be positioned on a wall or roof slope fronting a road or public footpath (or waterway in the Broads).

The dimensions given relate to the dish only, and exclude fixings, brackets etc.

Satellite Dishes on Flats

For larger blocks of flats (ie over 15m in height or approximately five stories) outside National Parks, Areas of Outstanding Natural Beauty, Conservation Areas or the Broads, two dishes in total are permitted for the whole block, each not to exceed 90cm. If the block is located within the above areas, then permission is required.

For smaller blocks of flats, one dish is permitted for the whole block.

Clearly once one or two people have erected a dish on a block of flats, then further dishes will require permission. In essence this means that erecting dishes on flats will often only be possible on a first come first served basis.

Running a Business/Working from Home

The planning situation regarding the use of a house for business purposes is not governed by simple legislation. A considerable amount of judgement is involved. The basic principle is that planning permission is not usually needed if the character and use of the building remains essentially residential. Planning permission <u>will</u> be needed if the character and use does <u>not</u> remain essentially residential.

Therefore it is usually possible, without planning permission, to:

* use part of a house to rent to a lodger or for bed and breakfast accommodation

* use a room as a personal office (for those who work from home)

* provide a small scale child minding service or playgroup

* use a room for a business such as music teaching, hairdressing, employment agency etc

* use a garage to repair cars occasionally or store goods connected with a business.

Clearly all the above activities could be carried out at widely different levels of intensity or scale. The use of a house without planning permission implies that the activities should be small scale and not cause disturbance. The following considerations will be important.

* The house should be used predominantly and substantially as a private domestic residence.

* There should not be a significant increase in traffic or visitors to the house. For instance an employment agency based on the phone may be acceptable, whilst one involving regular visitors would require permission.

* The business should not involve any activities out of place in a residential area, so disturbing neighbours by creating noise or smells.

* Generally speaking if anyone other than the residents of the house are being employed in the business then permission may be needed.

The basic test as to whether working from home will require permission is whether the changes in activity involved would be disruptive in a residential area. If not, and the house remains predominantly residential, then permission will not usually be needed.

A business started at home without requiring planning permission may go on to expand and prosper. So the level of activity will rise until the point is reached when it could be argued that planning permission is required. A pragmatic way of dealing with this could be to let the local Planning Department make the decision for you. Once they start receiving complaints etc they will contact you to request an application or instruct you to stop. Government advice is that businesses should not be excluded from residential areas without good reason, so you may be wise in pursuing your case to appeal. It would not be an offence to continue carrying on the business until the result of the appeal is issued unless the Local Authority have served a Stop Notice upon you. (See page 82).

— ◆ —

Granny Annexes

There is really no difference in planning terms between an extension to be used as a granny annexe and one used for additional bedrooms or other rooms of the house. Therefore if enough accommodation can be created using permitted development rights then it can be used as a granny annexe. If an extension of a substantial size is required, beyond the permitted limits, then planning permission will be needed - whether it will be used as a granny annexe or simply as additional bedrooms etc will not be an issue effecting its acceptability as a proposal.

The crucial point is that planning permission is required to create a separate and independent dwelling either by way of an extension or subdivision of the house. Whatever is built to house an elderly relative must therefore be an 'annexe' in the sense of being used only in connection with the main house. This would usually mean being physically accessible internally from the existing house. It may be possible to build a granny annexe in the garden, see the section on 'Outbuildings' on page 12.

— ◆ —

Shared Houses

Planning permission will not normally be required to use a house to provide rented accommodation, for instance, to students. However, the number of people living together must not exceed six. They must also, to quote the legislation, be living together "as a family", sharing facilities such as kitchens, bathrooms, sitting rooms, etc. If the number exceeds six or self contained bedsits are created, then planning permission may be required for a change of use.

◆

Maintenance and Repairs

Planning permission does not need to be obtained for the following:

* Internal alterations.

* Repairs and maintenance. This includes re-roofing a house, provided that there is no change in the shape or height.

* The insertion of new doors, windows or roof-lights. The right to create new windows gives rise to the anomaly that although planning permission would not normally be granted for an overlooking window as part of a new extension, once it is built permission is not required to then insert new windows. Provided of course that a condition is not attached to prohibit them.

* Painting or decorating the outside of the house. If a house is located in any of the areas listed in Designated Areas on page 8, then planning permission is required to clad the outside with stone, tile, artificial stone, plastic or timber. Elsewhere permission is not required to do this.

◆

Demolition and Re-building

* **demolition**

    Planning permission is not required to demolish any building of less than 50 cubic metres (measured externally). The demolition of any building used on a dwelling or attached to a dwelling which exceeds this size may require a plannning application. I would recommend that if you wish to demolish all or part of a house, that you provide details of what you intend and seek the advice of your local Planning Department.

* **demolition in Conservation Areas**

    'Conservation Area Consent' is required for most demolition works carried out in Conservation Areas. I would therefore recommend that you provide details of what you intend to demolish and seek the advice of your local Planning Department.

*   **re-building**

    If a building is demolished and it is intended to re-build it, in exactly the same form, planning permission is still required. What is more, it will not necessarily be granted. The proposed new building will be judged as if it were any other new proposal. If the original building caused the problems of overlooking or overshadowing or looked ugly, the planners are likely to want to improve matters.

———— ◆ ————

Written Confirmation

If, having considered this section you think that what you want to do is permitted development, then write to your Local Planning Authority, and request written confirmation that planning permission is not required. This is very important for peace of mind, to demonstrate to neighbours that everything is in order and to provide evidence when selling your house that the extensions or alterations made were legitimate. In your letter provide the following information (if you have it and it is relevant in your case):

*   your address
*   whether your house has been extended (since 1st July 1948)
*   whether your house is a terraced house
*   the size and position of the building you wish to construct
*   whether the proposed building will be within 2m of your garden boundary
*   whether the proposed extension would be within 5m of any existing outbuilding (or vice versa).

It is often helpful to provide some of the information in the form of a sketch, indicating the relevant distances between house, outbuildings, road, boundary etc in metres.

If the proposal is not considered to be permitted development, find out from the planning office exactly why not. It may be that minor adjustments to the size or position of the proposal would be sufficient to render it permitted development.

———— ◆ ————

Certificates of Lawful Use or Development

There is a procedure for obtaining from your local Planning Department a 'Certificate of Lawful Use or Development' (LDC). This constitutes a formal and legally binding decision by the Local Authority that a particular proposed or existing use or development does not require planning permission and is lawful. Its effects are similar to a planning permission and Conditions may be attached.

I would expect an LDC to be required only in special circumstances, for example where an applicant and the Local Authority are in dispute. If you become involved in applying for an LDC I recommend that you employ a fully qualified planning consultant. (For further information see Circular 17/92 and Section 10 of the Planning and Compensation Act 1991).

———— ◆ ————

Chapter 3

SUBMITTING A PLANNING APPLICATION

Chapter 3
SUBMITTING A PLANNING APPLICATION

The Procedure

The processing of your application will involve the following stages:

1. The application will be checked to ensure that forms are properly completed, plans included, the owner and/or leaseholder of the property (if not yourself) notified and the correct fee paid.

2. If all is correct the application will be 'registered' and allocated a number.

3. The application will be advertised to ensure that people know about it. This may involve some or all of the following: newspaper adverts, notices placed on the site of the proposal, individual letters sent to neighbours. The site notice must be in placed for at least 21 days and it is the reponsibility of the planning authority to erect it, although they may well request that the applicant does this.

4. Consultations will be carried out. This will include notifying the Parish or Town Council, the local highways authority, and other public bodies who supply services such as water or drainage.

5. A Planning Officer will be allocated your application. He or she will consider it against existing Council policies and any past history of decisions relating to your house or similar houses in the area. The Council will often have standards which will need to be satisfied for things like parking provision, visibility near road junctions etc.

6. The Planning Officer will visit the site.

7. The Planning Officer will make a recommendation of refusal or approval. He or she may request changes to the proposal if they feel problems can be overcome - although you cannot always depend on this helpful approach.

8. The decision will be made by the Chief Officer responsible for planning matters, or the application will be considered by a Planning Committee made up of local Councillors. If objections are raised to the application by neighbours or anyone else it would generally be reported to a committee. The Planning Committee may wish to make a site visit, and the decision will then be made at the next meeting following that visit.

9. Once the application has been determined you will receive a decision notice.

How Long Does It Take?

Local Authorities have a duty under the legislation to determine applications within eight weeks. In practice, different Planning Departments have varying degrees of success in working within this time limit.

Unless amended plans are required, most householder applications should be expected to be determined within the eight week period.

————————— ♦ —————————

Before You Submit The Application

Planning applications are supposed to be dealt with within eight weeks of registration. Overcoming objections by talking to your neighbours and ensuring that the design and appearance of your proposal is satisfactory to the planners is the most effective way of reducing the time and hassle involved in the process.

A planning application is likely to be most successful if the Planners are considered as one of the team involved in the development proposal. The team is made up of you the Applicant, the person drawing the plans and the Planner. The person who draws up the proposal is faced with the task of reconciling the sometimes conflicting requirements of the Applicant, Planner and Building Regulations.

The following advice may be helpful in reducing the likelihood of delay or of a refusal.

*   When you have decided roughly what you wish to do, whether it is an extension, new garage, moving your boundary fence or whatever, take relevant photographs of your house, draw some rough sketches and make an appointment to discuss the proposals with a Planning Officer. You will receive informal verbal advice as to the likely acceptability of what you wish to do. This is the stage at which complete non-starters may be eliminated.

*   It is best that the pre-application advice is only obtained in <u>verbal</u> form. Informal <u>written</u> comments are likely to be less flexible and may amount to a hasty, partial assessment of your proposal. This could have an influence upon the formal consideration of the actual planning application. You may be tempted to leave a copy of your sketch proposal for the Planning Officer to consider. However, this is not advisable because the sketch is unlikely to be an accurate or sophisticated representation of what is desired and could lead to an unnecessarily negative response. A <u>site meeting</u> to discuss your proposal is probably the best method of gauging the likelihood of an approval. Unfortunately, not all Planning Authorities have the resources to provide such a service. Photographs offer a reasonable alternative.

Consider carefully the advice you have received. Either draw the plans yourself or instruct someone else to do them for you. You may wish to use an agent to act on your behalf or you can deal with the Planners personally (see page 5).

————————— ♦ —————————

Submitting the Application

*   The application will not be registered unless it is complete and the forms correctly filled in. At this stage, telephone the Planning Department to find out when it would be convenient to have your application checked by a Planning Officer. Having the application checked prior to submission saves time involved in amending anything once it has been received. The application is checked for its completeness - no judgement is made as to its acceptability as a proposal.

*   Once you have been informed that the application is registered keep a note of the application number and find out the name of the Planning Officer who is dealing with it.

*   You should feel free to contact the Planning Officer handling your case to discuss its progress and to give any additional information needed. (Try not to pester the Planning Officers though and wait for a few weeks after you have submitted the application before you contact them). Amendments to the design or siting may be required to make a proposal acceptable. Try to ensure that these are provided rather than let the application be refused - some authorities do not like negotiating once an application has been submitted due to the time involved. However, it would be unreasonable of them not to explain the nature of any problems if you contact them, so giving you an opportunity to amend the proposal accordingly.

*   It may happen that despite the informal advice you received initially, and your willingness to make minor revisions to the proposal, your plan is recommended for refusal. Find out exactly what the problem is. If the application is certain to be recommended for refusal then it may be sensible to <u>withdraw</u> it prior to the day of the Committee. This will enable you to start the negotiations afresh. Withdrawing the application does prevent a Refusal Notice being issued which could devalue your property and perhaps prejudice future negotiations or consideration by the Committee.

*   Don't start work until you have actually received the permission notice. Remembear that anything anybody says during the whole procedure carries no actual weight in terms of the decision until you have actually got the written decision notices in your hands. This can be extremely frustrating. Whatever advice you receive from the Planning Officer dealing with your application, the Councillors or the Chief Planning Officer may wish to overrule it, and they may legitimately do so.

If your application is refused, reasons will be given and you must decide whether or not to appeal against this (see Chapter 5). If it is approved, conditions will often be attached (see page 30).

———— ◆ ————

The Role of Councillors

Parish Councils/Town Councils

In some Districts, particularly in rural areas, there are Parish Councils (in Scotland and Wales these are called community Councils) and Town Councils. These groups of elected Councillors do <u>not</u> have any planning powers, but they are usually consulted about planning applications and make observations on their own or their parishioners' behalf. Just because they don't object does not mean an application will be approved by the District or vice-versa. As a point of interest, many such Councillors are not elected, they simply stand unopposed. The District Councils do take note of what Parish or Town Councils have to say. If they object an application will usually need to go before the Planning Committee in the same way as if a neighbour were to object. Therefore it is often worth attempting to forestall such objections by talking to the Parish Councillors about what you wish to do.

Borough/District Councillors - your democratic representatives

Two things worth remembering:

1.   The Councillors on the Planning Committees, or Planning Officers acting on their behalf, make the decisions on planning applications.

2.   The Planning Officers make decisions on behalf of the Councillors. The Councillors are <u>your</u> elected representatives.

This knowledge may be helpful in a number of ways.

*   If you know that a neighbour objects strongly to your proposal and has been lobbying the members of the Planning Committee, it may be worth talking to your local Councillor, particularly if he or she is a also a member of the Planning Committee. Be careful not to be too pushy however, as too much pestering and lobbying may end up being counter productive.

*   If you are advised that your application is to be refused under delegated authority it may be worth requesting that it is considered by the Committee. Pursuading them to make a Committee Site Visit could also ensure that your proposal gets a fair and full consideration.

*   If your neighbours raise strong objections to what you wish to do, they may persuade the Councillors to refuse your application against the advice of the Planning Officers. In these circumstances (time permitting) it could be well worth appealing against a refusal.

──────── ◆ ────────

Types of Application

A Householder application for a straight forward domestic extension, garages or whatever will be a <u>full</u> application which means it provides all the details of what is proposed. The different types of application are described below.

1.   Full applications: If you wish to seek approval for both the principle and details of a proposal. (Full permission is always required if you wish to make a "change of use" application. For instance, to change a house into a shop).

2.   Outline applications: If you wish to know only whether a development would be acceptable in principle. More detailed matters can be reserved for subsequent approval. Outline permission lasts for 5 years but the reserved matters must be submitted within 3 years of the date it was granted. If they are not submitted within 3 years the outline permission cannot be implemented.

3.   Approval of reserved matters: Where outline permission has already been granted, but you wish to apply for approval of the detailed reserved matters.

4.   Temporary permission: If you require approval for change of use or other works for a specific short-term period only.

5.   Relaxation of conditions: If you wish to apply to relax a condition or conditions of a previous permission.

6.   Renewal of planning permission: A planning permission can only be renewed where consent has not expired - no plans required (just fee and ownership certificate with covering letter).

The Planning Application Itself

A planning application consists of a set of completed application forms (provided by the Planning Department) and a set of plans of the proposal (provided by you) and the appropriate fee.

The Fee

The current fee (July 1992) charged by Local Planning Authorities is £55 for an application for an extension or other domestic proposal.

The Application Forms

Planning Departments tend to have their own design of application forms, but the questions asked are similar. Some departments provide simplified application forms used in householder applications only. An example of such a form is shown in the Appendix. I have considered each question in turn.

Questions 1 and 2
Name and Address of Applicant and Agent

I recommend that you complete these forms yourself. If you encounter difficulties then the Planning Department will help you to avoid confusion.

If the name and address of an agent is given, all correspondence from the department will be sent to that agent. It will be useful to give a contact name. In the absence of any agent, remember to give your daytime telephone number.

Question 3
Site Address

This will usually be your address, but remember that you can make a planning application in relation to property which you do not own. This is helpful should you wish to buy a house but want to make the purchase subject to a successful application to extend it.

Question 4
What is the Application for?

This should be a clear, simple description of what is proposed. Describe the number of storeys and the position in relation to the existing house (rear, side or front).

Examples:

*   single storey detached garage in rear garden
*   two storey side extension
*   front facing pitched roofed dormer window

Question 5
Plans and Drawings

The type of plans and drawings which are required are considered in detail below. On the forms you should describe the type of plan and its scale.

For example: location plan (1:1250), site plan (1:500) and elevations (1:100).

Question 6
Will the proposed materials match the existing?

The answer to this should normally be yes.

Question 7
Is the site boundary to be altered?

If you wish to increase the size of your garden area by enclosing agricultural land or by enclosing an area of public open space provided on a housing estate, then this will in itself require planning permission. So if the answer to this question is yes, it should usually be reflected in question 4. If in doubt, ask the Planning Department.

Question 8
Drainage

All new buildings containing new kitchens or bathrooms should have separate connections to the foul water sewer, and all new roofs connections to a storm water sewer. Therefore before you start, locate the position of the nearest drains and sewers, building over them creates problems which can be very expensive. The building regulations department of the local Council should be able to advise you on this.

Question 9
Are there any trees to be felled?

Planning authorities will wish to see trees retained wherever possible. You would be wise to investigate whether any trees you wish to remove are protected by a Tree Preservation Order or previous planning condition, or because they are in a Conservation Area. If the Planning Authority considers an attractive tree is threatened, then they can serve an emergency TPO. Remember that special kinds of foundations can be laid which will not damage tree roots and which will not be damaged by them. Removing large trees can often cause more structural damage than retaining them.

Question 10
Access (see Permitted Development - Chapter 2 Page 15)

If you need a new vehicle access from a road onto your property across a pavement, then a pavement crossover and dropped kerb must be constructed at your expense to the Council's specifications.

Question 11
Fees

A fee is charged by the Council for dealing with the application. It is not refunded if permission is refused or if the application is withdrawn!

———— ◆ ————

Ownership Certificate

When making a planning application you must complete and sign a certificate provided with the forms which states the ownership of the property. This is known as a section 66 certificate. If you do not own the property then you must serve the notice (which must be detached from the certificate) on the owner. This is a legal requirement and is irrespective of whether they already know about the application. A permission granted for an application with an incorrect certificate of ownership may be open to challenge if it can be demonstrated that the other owner of the land was seriously disadvantaged by the omission. A dishonest certificate can incur a fine. This certificate seems to cause endless problems and is often the cause of a delay in the registering of an application. So if you don't understand it phone up the Planning Department and ask their help in filling it in.

———— ◆ ————

The Plans

The following plans will be required, with all dimensions scaled and in metric. Examples are provided in the Appendix, "Model Applications". Most planning authorities will require four copies of all the plans and four sets of completed application forms.

1. **Location Plan** (scale 1:1250)

    This is to show the location of your house and its position in relation to the surrounding roads. This is to help the Planning Officer and any other interested persons to find the house! Many Planning Departments are able to provide copies of suitable location plans for a reasonable price.

2. **Site Plan** (scale 1:500)

    This should show clearly and accurately the application site (marked with a red line), the position of north, the footprint of the house with the proposed extensions drawn on it, and the position and footprint of all houses and roads directly bordering the site and all other buildings (such as garages and sheds) on the application site. (See examples in Appendix).

3. **Floor Plans** (scale 1:100 or 1:50)

    These should show the layout of rooms of both existing and proposed parts of the house. However, there is clearly no need to show the upstairs floor layout when applying for a single storey extension.

4. **Elevations** (scale 1:100 or 1:50)

    These are drawings of what the house will look like from the outside, with notation indicating what materials are to be used. It should be made clear on these drawings what is existing and what is proposed. There is no point in showing areas of the house which are not affected by the proposal.

———— ◆ ————

Existing Plans

If your house was built after 1947 or it has been extended since that date, then your Planning Department should have copies of the original plans of the house. Copies will quite often be made available for you to purchase. Obtaining copies of these plans can save a significant amount of money if you have a complete set of plans drawn up, or time, if you intend to do the plans yourself.

NB: These plans are themselves copyright, but you could use them as the basis of your own application.

———— ◆ ————

The Application Site

This is the area of land which contains the property involved in the application. In a householder application this will simply be the whole of the garden containing the house (known in planning jargon as the curtilage of the dwelling). It is important that a red line is drawn around the curtilage on the site plan because this line represents the legally binding definition of the site to which the application relates. The red line needs to be drawn on all four copies of the site plan or the application will not be registered.

◆

What Sort of Decision can be made?

1.   Your application may be approved. It will usually be approved subject to certain conditions. In some areas a copy of the plans that have been approved are sent back to the applicant so that there can be no doubt as to what has been agreed.

2.   Your application may be refused. If so, the reasons will be listed on the decision notice.

3.   Your application may be approved subject to you entering into a legally binding agreement regarding a particular aspect of the proposal. For instance in order to provide a drainage system or highway improvements. This agreement will relate to the property not just to the person who enters into it.

      (Some Authorities will resolve to grant permission following the completion of the agreement. Others only resolve to authorise the Chief Planner to grant permission following the agreement. In the latter case the Authority have still got the right not to grant permission should circumstances change between the consideration of the application and signing of the agreement).

◆

Conditions

There is always a condition on a grant of planning permission that the development permitted must commence within a certain period of time. For a full permission this is usually five years. There are rarely conditions which demand that the development should be completed within a certain time. This means that in most cases once a development has been started the permission cannot expire. A development will normally be considered to have been started once foundation work has commenced in accordance with the necessary building regulations.

When planning permission is granted, there will often be conditions attached to the approval - things which enable the permission to be granted. An example would be the condition that the materials used should match the existing materials; the permission would not be granted if the extension were to be built in bricks or roof tiles which look terrible next to the existing house. Another common condition is that there should be adequate car parking available, where for instance there are on street parking problems. If you are unclear what any condition means, ask the Planning Department.

You may appeal against conditions which you feel are unreasonable (see Chapter 5). However, in so doing you are opening up the entire permission for reconsideration and ultimately the whole thing could be refused.

Some conditions will demand that you do certain things (such as plant trees) 'to the Local Planning Authority's satisfaction'. In these cases and others where it is not clear exactly what is required, get agreement in writing from the Planning Department that each condition has been met after you have finished the work (or before if necessary). This is in your interest, as you can be fined for failure to implement conditions.

Making an Application on Land you do not own

It is quite in order for someone to make a planning application on land which does not belong to them and over which they have no control, provided that they notify in writing the actual owner of the land. This notification is done by means of a particular form called a Section 66 certificate, which must be completed when submitting a planning application.
This ability does give rise to confusion and people sometimes feel intimidated or offended if they are informed that someone is seeking permission on their land. However, gaining planning permission has no influence whatsoever over land ownership or the control of land. Just because a developer gains planning permission to build a house in your garden does not influence the fact that it is your garden. What is more, planning permission relates to the land (or buildings) not to the applicant (unless it is specifically personal consent, which is rare). This means you may implement a permission relating to your house which was gained by another person, eg a previous owner.

Applications Affecting Boundaries

You require your neighbours' consent to build on their land, which includes foundations and overhanging eaves, guttering or downpipes. You will also need their consent to enter their land to enable buildings on or close to the boundary to be built. It is sometimes possible to build from within a site, but it is simpler and probably quicker to have all round access.

The ownership and alignment of property boundaries is shown on deeds, usually held by mortgage companies.

Permission will be needed for the use of a neighbour's wall to tie into, or building an extension where a wall is not in joint ownership. Remember planning permission does not remove any other legal duties regarding ownership or access rights.

Land Ownership

To ascertain the ownership of land is usually a simple matter. (Although this is not always the case as not all land is registered). The land registry records are open to the public and filling in a form sent with the appropriate fee will provide the required information. To obtain the address of the relevant land registry for your area telephone the Land Charges section of your local Council.

◆

Planning Application Checklist

Have you had the informal view of the local Planning Department on your proposal? Is it positive?

Have you talked to your neighbour about your proposal, and checked the situation regarding the ownership of boundaries etc?

Have you provided four copies of a location plan showing the application site outlined in red?

Have you provided four copies of the application forms and all relevant elevations and floor plans?

Have you filled in the ownership certificate correctly (if in any doubt check with the Planning Department) or served notice on any other property owner who is affected?

Have you checked whether any trees will be affected, if so, are they protected by a TPO?

Have you checked your deeds for any restrictive covenants which will be affected?

Is the correct fee attached to the forms?

Have you signed the forms and certificates?

Have you kept a copy of everything for your own information?

◆

Chapter 4

WHAT WILL GET PLANNING PERMISSION?

Chapter 4
WHAT WILL GET PLANNING PERMISSION?

This chapter is intended to help you decide whether what you want to do to your home is likely to receive planning permission. It should also be useful in suggesting other ideas and possibilities which you might not have considered.

◆

Planning – an Art Not a Science

There are no hard or fast rules determining what will or won't receive planning permission. Exactly the same proposal may be perfectly acceptable in one location but be refused in another.

Not all Planning Authorities adopt the same policies and in different areas of the country certain aspects of a proposal may be considered more important than others.

The advice in this chapter will indicate what sort of concerns the Planners are likely to have and should enable you to speak to them on their own terms. Planning permission for even small extensions will sometimes be the result of negotiation and compromise between the homeowner and planner. Understanding the issues involved should enable you to work <u>with</u> him/her rather than against him/her. There will usually be a number of design solutions to any one planning problem.

◆

A Major Investment

Some of the suggestions made in this Chapter may result in an extension being more expensive to build. However:

* A poorly designed extension is unlikely to receive planning permission.

* If it does, a poorly designed extension may well add little or no value to your property and could make it more diffucult to sell.

In the case of a well designed and attractive extension the reverse of the above is likely to be true. Any proposal is likely to be a major investment of your money, so it is worth doing well.

◆

General Principles

Householder Planning Applications are likely to be considered from two separate angles, the Planner will be concerned about:

* the effect of the proposal upon the living environment of neighbouring properties;

* the look of the proposal and the effect it will have on the appearance of the surrounding area. (Bearing in mind any special characteristics of the house and its locality and any relevant planning policies).

In making these judgements, the Planner will apply a variety of general principles which are explained in this chapter and should be a useful guide as to what is likely to be acceptable. Before looking at these principles it is important to be aware of certain policy designations which could affect the overall level of control which may be imposed.

Areas which have Special Designations

If your house is located in an area which has a special designation in planning policy terms, then the level of scrutiny which your proposal will be subjected to will be greatly increased. Such areas are:

* Green belts
* National Parks
* Areas of Outstanding Natural Beauty
* Norfolk Broads
* Conservation Areas
* Areas of special character

I will consider each in turn.

Green Belts

Areas of land around a large number of towns and cities are designated as 'Green Belt'. The specific purpose of this designation is to prevent these towns and cities from expanding continually into the open countryside which surrounds them. The general policy applied to land within the Green Belt is to prevent, as far as possible, all new development. There are a limited number of exceptions to this policy, such as development required for agriculture. Applications for house extensions in the open countryside or in villages within the Green Belt are likely to receive very careful consideration in terms of their visual and physical impact upon the open and undeveloped character of their surroundings.

Conservation Areas

Local Planning Authorities will designate some areas of towns and villages as Conservation Areas. These are defined in the legislation as 'areas of special architectural interest the character and appearance of which it is desirable to preserve or enhance'. The principle legal effects of designation are that most forms of building demolition require consent (Conservation Area Consent), and that anyone proposing to fell or work on a tree must inform the Local Planning Authority six weeks in advance. Failure to accord with either of these stipulations is an offence. Permitted development rights are also reduced. The consideration of all planning applications within Conservation Areas will be specially thorough and excellent standards of design and materials will be demanded. The basic test being that any new development must 'preserve and enhance the character of the Conservation Area'.

Emphasis will be given to the traditional styles, materials and design details found within the Conservation Area.

National Parks, Areas of Outstanding Natural Beauty and the Norfolk Broads

These three designations are given in recognition of the special landscape qualities and natural beauty of these areas. In planning terms such areas are considered highly sensitive to developments of any kind. So special scrutiny will be given to design, materials, visual prominence etc, and the traditional local architecture will be valued. Permitted development rights are reduced and this is a reflection of the perceived importance of controlling inappropriate development.

Areas of Special Character

Many planning authorities have identified in their 'Local Plans' parts of towns and villages, which are not suitable for Conservation Area status, but have a special character considered worthy of preservation. This designation may be given to all kinds of areas, from leafy suburbia to Victorian terraced houses. If you find out what 'special character' has been identified you will have a sporting chance of meeting the planners' requirements.

———— ◆ ————

Other Considerations

Precedent

All planning applications are supposed to be considered 'on their merits', i.e. individually and without prejudice. On the other hand, planning authorities do attempt to be consistent and it would be unreasonable if two very similar proposals received very different decisions. This means that when a planning application is being considered, precedent will be an issue. The consequence for homeowner applications is that in addition to the issues involved in a particular case, the planner will ask himself "what if everybody were to do this?"

Security

The design of an extension or position of a fence may effect the vulnerability of a house to burglary.

Trees and Shrubs

The quality and quantity of existing planting in a garden will have a crucial effect upon the potential appearance of any new extension or major alteration to a house. Try to keep as many existing trees and shrubs as possible when extending. The planners will wish to see them retained to maintain the setting of the house and street. They often attach conditions to ensure this and to ensure that additional trees are planted.

◆

The Basic Principles

This section deals with questions of neighbourliness and the protection of residential environments and also with issues of good design and the character of an area.

1. Neighbourliness

This is a first priority and means protecting the residential environments of neighbouring properties, ensuring that what you build does not cause serious loss of sunlight or privacy.

Overlooking

The more closely spaced houses are, the more important it is to consider privacy in the design of an extension. Privacy may be lost through the construction of an extension which allows views into the windows of a neighbouring property, or into a nearby private rear garden. Overlooking may also be caused by balconies, roof gardens or first floor conservatories.

Windows which cause an unacceptable degree of overlooking will not be permitted. In most cases this means that there should be no first floor windows on the sides of houses other than obscure glazed landing or bathroom windows. The key phrase to note here is 'unacceptable degree of overlooking'. This is because what is classified as 'overlooking' will usually depend upon window to boundary and window to window distances. Where windows currently overlook a neighbour, the addition of new ones on the same elevation is unlikely to be a problem.

Window to Window Distances

There is a generally acknowledged requirement of a minimum 'privacy distance' of 21m (70 feet) between facing first floor windows. Ground floor windows are rarely a problem unless differences in ground levels cause them to be elevated above fence level. Extensions which would bring windows closer than this distance will not be acceptable. In situations where houses do not directly face on another, then the minimum window to window distance may be reduced, because the problem of direct overlooking from one window to another may not occur.

Standards of what may be considered 'acceptable' levels of privacy are likely to be increased in locations where high levels of privacy are the norm. For instance, in an area of secluded detached houses in large plots it would not be appropriate to allow an overlooking window on a neighbouring extension simply because the minimum 21m window to window distance was being complied with.

Window to Boundary Distances

The overlooking of neighbouring rear gardens is undesirable and should be avoided. A first floor primary window will usually be considered to cause unacceptable overlooking if it is closer than $10^{1}/2$m to the boundary of the neighbours garden. This represents half the 21m window to window distance described above and it is a minimum. In situations when neighbouring gardens are entirely private then the windows in a new extension should be positioned to avoid causing any overlooking at all.

Overshadowing

Most people value very highly the amount of sunlight and daylight which comes through their windows. So it is important that extensions do not overshadow neighbouring windows or cause a serious loss of sunlight. However, as always it is a matter of the degree of overshadowing. Due to the movement of the sun, some windows are more or less likely to be overshadowed or to lose direct sunlight. Therefore a rear extension may be permitted in one instance but not in another due to the orientation of the houses.

- *A two storey rear extension built right on the boundary. This is likely to be acceptable in terms of overshadowing, it does not overlook and fits well with the design of the existing house. Planning permission is therefore likely to be granted. However, the overhanging roof and gutters and foundations are over the neighbouring property, the owners written permission will therefore be needed.*

- *A full width single storey rear extension like this is the kind of addition which can often be built without planning permission. (See Chapter 2). However, the permission of the neighbouring property owner will be required if either the foundations or gutters are built over the neighbour's land.*

The Movement of the Sun

If you live in the house you wish to extend then you will have accurate knowledge of the sun's movement during the day. You are therefore in a good position to judge what effect your extension would have on the neighbouring house. Remember that just because the neighbour is happy with your ideas does not mean that the planner will be. It is their job to protect the residential environment of houses, not just their owners at any particular time.

◆

The 45° Rule

A useful guideline which is adopted by many planners is the 45° rule. This is intended to prevent extensions having an overshadowing, dominating and overbearing effect on neighbouring properties. To comply with this rule an extension should not extend beyond a line drawn at an angle of 45° from the nearest edge of the nearest window of the neighbouring house, excluding such things as bathroom, utility room or landing windows. For one or two storey extensions the line should be drawn from the nearest ground floor or first floor window. Generally speaking a stricter approach will be taken when dealing with two storey extensions than single storey ones because the potential for overshadowing is greater.

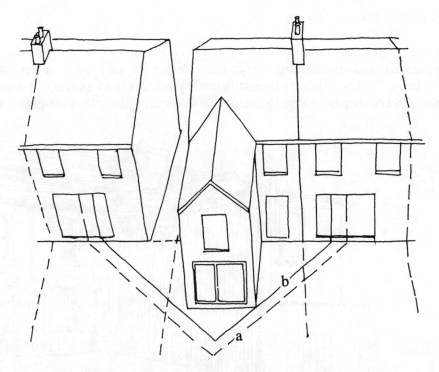

• *This diagram shows a fairly sophisticated version of the 45° rule which is used by some planning authorities. The dotted line (a) indicates the line measured from halfway across the nearest window which single storey extensions should not cross. The line (b) shows the line from a quarter of the window width which two storey extension should not cross.*

This 45° rule will not usually be applied rigidly as many other factors can be involved. For instance if the rear of a house already has very limited access to daylight or sunlight then even a neighbouring extension which meets the 45° rule can have an unacceptable effect. In some cases even small one or two storey extensions can cause serious overshadowing due to the design of neighbouring houses and the sun's position. Due to the movement of the sun an extension which breaks the 45° rule may be acceptable because loss of sunlight does not occur.

• *This drawing shows an extension which meets the basic 45° rule measured from the edge of the neighbour's downstairs window. However, the movement of the sun also needs to be considered to avoid too serious loss of sunlight.*

Oppressiveness

An extension or outbuilding may not overshadow or overlook, but it may have an oppressive and overbearing effect on a neighbour and create a poor aspect from their windows. This is difficult to quantify but if you think the visual effect would be to dominate the neighbouring house and garden then it is quite likely that the planners won't like it.

• *Over large rear extensions can cause an oppressive environment and serious overshadowing of a neighbour's garden and windows. This extension causes both these things and also looks horrible!*

Permitted Development

A significant amount of development may be built using permitted development rights. Such development is likely to have some effect in terms of overshadowing etc. For example, a 2m high wall or 3m high enclosure would have some impact on a neighbouring garden. An extension would usually need to cause appreciably more harm than these permitted developments, to justify a refusal.

◆

2. Good Design and the Character of an Area

There is a great deal of debate about how much planners should concern themselves in questions of good and bad design. There is a fine line between personal opinions about what is and is not attractive and professional judgements about what is or is not 'in character' with a house and its surroundings. There is general agreement that planners should not concern themselves with matters of personal preference.

To understand the approach taken by most planners it is useful to consider <u>poor design</u> simply as <u>a lack of design</u>. Where there has clearly been no thought put into the appearance of a proposal and no attempt has been made to respect the character of an existing building or its surroundings, then this may fairly be described by the Planners as bad design.

This does not mean that just because something is different that it is undesirable or it should be refused. Particularly when a house or its surroundings has no special character or features which can be identified by the planners as being of particular value or worthy of preservation.

◆

3. Extensions

This section will consider different kinds of extensions, drawing attention to relevant planning issues where appropriate.

Front Extensions

There is considerable scope on many houses for a front extension of moderate or small size. Extending the front of a house may be useful in providing a larger lounge, large porch, downstairs WC or even additional bedrooms. However the front of the house is likely to be visually the most sensitive and prominent part, and changes to it need to be considered carefully.

• *A typical small recently built three bed detached house with single garage attached to one side.*

• *Extending it across the front to create a bay window, covered porch and lengthened garage enables an additional bedroom above the garage and utility room to the rear. The design remains in keeping with the house, and neighbours are not overshadowed, overlooked or in any way badly affected, so provided that adequate parking is available it is unlikely that there would be a problem obtaining planning permission.*

The Building Line

The building line often seems to be the only piece of planning jargon people have heard of, but it is only of limited significance. Conformity with the 'building line' in a street becomes more important, the more rigidly it has been complied with in the past. This means that in areas where all the houses are a similar distance to the road, then building in front of this line would be very apparent and change the appearance of the area. In less regimented areas where many houses have different relationships with each other and are set at different distances from the road, or have substantial front gardens, then there is likely to be more flexibility and potential to build forward of the existing building line.

• *A carefully designed front and side extension which incorporates a new garage. It utilises the L shaped front of the house to provide a porch and WC which do not project forward of the existing building.*

The design of some houses will enable quite large and substantial front extensions, particularly where a house is designed in an 'L' shape. Filling in the 'L' is often quite acceptable because the extension will come no closer to the road than the existing house and neighbours are unlikely to suffer harm.

◆

Side Extensions

Extending at the side of a house is very common - examples of both single storey and two storey side extensions may be seen in most residential areas.

The Character of the Area

The infilling of gaps between houses can have a radical effect on the appearance of a street. Many planning authorities adopt the rule that no two storey extensions should come within one metre of a shared boundary. However, this in itself is arbitrary, and will in many cases be insufficient. A larger gap is likely to be required on the edge of towns or in rural areas where it is necessary to maintain greater space between buildings in order to preserve the spacious character of an area. The best guide to the size of side extension which would be permitted is to consider the general layout of houses in the road. Single storey side extensions are not usually considered a problem in this respect, as the gap between houses will still be apparent.

- *This shows the previous gap between two houses. Such large extensions close to a shared boundary are unlikely to be unacceptable when the resulting "terrace effect" is contrary to the existing character of an area. Large set backs at second storey level (as shown on the left) can sometimes be used to overcome this problem.*

Terracing Effect

Terracing effect is a phrase used to denote the effect of infilling gaps between previously semi-detached or detached houses, producing what appears to be a continually built-up frontage. It tends to be very unpopular with people who feel that their houses are devalued because of the actions of neighbours, although such devaluation is not a planning matter. Building bedrooms above garages is a popular form of extension on modern estates where the design of houses often lend themselves to this type of change. However, the terrace effect will be considered undesirable, particularly if in any particular road it has not yet occurred. Once such extensions are permitted in a street, it becomes progressively more difficult for planners to resist similar ones.

• *A bulky side extension which is out of character with the house. This is entirely unacceptable.*

• *An extension which is only marginally smaller in actual floor area but which relates much better to the existing house. The window size, roof design and small set back all improve its appearance. (The side window could be a problem in terms of overlooking unless it faces a blank wall, is obscure glazed or this is on a corner plot).*

Joining The Old With The New

The best means of providing a clean join between the old and the new is to ensure that the extension is set back from the front of the house, as above.

There are two major benefits of setting back the new extension like this:

(1) It is practically impossible other than with extremely recent houses to get an exact match between old and new bricks or other materials. Setting back avoids a scruffy and mismatched join and creates a neat appearance regardless of the precise match of materials.

(2) A set back helps to ensure that the original building keeps its essential character and design after the extension has been added. For example, a matched pair of semi-detached houses can sometimes be spoilt in appearance if a large extension to one is allowed to 'unbalance' the pair.

It is possible to extend successfully at the side without a set back, if for instance the house is rendered or painted; the extension wraps around the front of the house at single storey level; or the original bricks and roof covering can still be obtained.

A substantial set back may be used to retain the appearance of a gap between houses whilst still enabling a two storey side extension close to the boundary.

- *An existing victorian detached house*

- *A two storey rear extension which appears over large and bulky, out of scale with the existing house. A bland and unattractive addition which would be unlikely to get planning permission.*

- *A two storey extension only marginally smaller than the one above. However, the roof is slightly lower than the main house, the side wall is set back a short distance, and the existing gable end remains unaffected. The result is an extension which appears far less bulky. It is in character with the existing house, and does not remove any existing attractive features. It is far more likely, therefore, to be granted planning permission.*

Roof Height and Shape on Side Extensions

The above illustrations also indicate the effect of an even slightly lowered roof height on the appearance of the extended house. In general a roof height lower than the original is desirable - it should certainly be no higher. Any set back on the front elevations should be carried through to the roof level. All two storey side extensions should have roofs of the same pitch as the original house, and have tiles or slates as near a match as possible to the original. Flat roofs will generally be frowned upon, and particularly those which are visible from a public area. Flat roofed extensions above single storey height, although approved in the past, are extremely unlikely to be approved today. See the example below:

- *Two storey flat roofed extensions are nearly always ugly and visually obtrusive, on a prominent corner site such as this the unattractive appearance is made even more obvious.*

Sometimes areas are characterised by the existence of flat roofed garages. In this kind of situation the planners would be unjustified in insisting on pitched roofs upon new single storey side extensions. Although sometimes cheaper to build, flat roofs often cost the same as pitched roofs and the latter usually need far less future maintenance. In the circumstances where a flat roofed side extension is the only option a false pitch to the front can be an acceptable compromise.

If you are considering building over an existing garage, check that the existing foundations are adequate to cope with the additional load before going to the expense of making a planning application.

Rear Extensions

Two Storey Rear Extensions

Potential harm caused by overlooking or overshadowing will need to be considered carefully. Irrespective of those problems some planning authorities seek to impose a maximum of three metres in depth upon rear extensions. In the case of terraced houses or small semi-detached houses this may be reasonable but otherwise such a restriction could be unjustified, particularly on a detached house with a large plot. In such a case it could be worthwhile appealing against a refusal, unless clear justification is provided by the Planning Authority, in terms of extremely unattractive design or harmful effects upon the residential environment of neighbouring houses. There is no reason why very large rear extensions cannot be acceptable in planning terms if the particular circumstances are right.

Roof Height and Shape on Two Storey Rear Extensions

As with other forms of extension, it is recommended that roof pitches should match the rest of the house and that the roof height should be set lower than the main ridge. Flat roofs are normally an eyesore and are best avoided. The height of a pitched roof can be reduced by the use of dormer windows or skylights which enable the roof space itself to be utilised. The height and physical bulk of a roof may also be reduced by using a hipped, twin gable or valley roof. Where the roof threatens to block out the sun, sloping it away from the affected neighbour can help to reduce the overshadowing effect. A part single storey, part two storey extension can often make the most of a restricted site.

- *This large two storey rear extension has been built using a valley roof. This can be constructed so that it does not create a maintenance liability. Its advantage is that it enables a very large extension across the full width of the house which leaves the style and character of the existing house basically the same.*

Single Storey Rear Extensions

Most houses are able to accommodate and benefit from some form of single storey rear extension. Provided that the materials used are suitable and the roof pitch is in keeping, then the possibility of a harmful impact on the appearance of the house is likely to be limited. Flat roofs, unless genuinely necessary to avoid harm to neighbours, should be avoided.

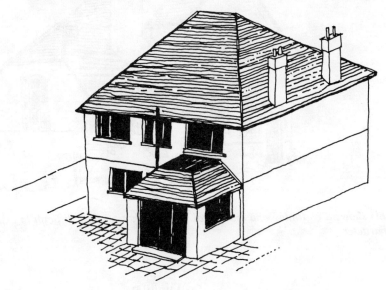

- *When a fully pitched roof cannot be built this style of roof is an acceptable compromise, and would be preferred to a flat roof.*

Overshadowing and overlooking are obviously less likely to be a problem than with a two storey extension. However, the proximity of neighbouring windows and the movement of the sun will still need to be considered. Overlooking could be a problem if a roof top patio were created or if there are different ground levels between neighbouring properties.

As a general rule, it is helpful not to build directly on the boundary and to keep the roof height low so that any effect on neighbours is minimised.

- *Both garage and porch match well with the style of the house because the same roof pitch and materials are used.*

Two Approaches to Extending a House

- *This shows a charming and individual victorian house. It is difficult to extend and retain its original character.*

- *This is a very poor proposal and spoils the style of the house and looks bulky and bland. Points to note are:*

  - *The roof pitch is shallower than the existing house*

  - *The extension partially hides the attractive chimney decoration*

  - *There is no set back or physical break between the old and new. This spoils the character of the existing house and increases the apparent bulk of the whole house. Also unless the match of old and new materials is perfect (which is unlikely) then the join could be scruffy*

  - *The large windows are entirely out of keeping with the older style of the existing windows*

  - *The width of the extension is out of scale with the width of the existing house*

- *This is a far better proposal whilst providing almost as much additional floorspace as the awful one considered above. This extension respects the style and character of the existing house. Note the setting back of the new bit; lower roof height and identical roof pitch; retention of existing decorative features on the chimney; and similar window sizes and style. A good compromise which is not bland and retains the overall sense of scale of the original victorian house.*

- *These drawings show traditional buildings which have been extended many years ago, the additions follow the general style, roof pitch and details of the main house. The existence of a series of extensions to old buildings is often what gives them the charm and character they have today.*

Garden Areas

Most planning authorities will have standards for desirable minimum private garden areas or minimum garden depths. This is to resist the overdevelopment of residential areas. Such garden area policies are usually flexible to some extent, but they need to be considered if you are proposing to extend but have only a small rear garden. The minimum depth of rear garden required is usually 10.5m.

◆

4. Roof Conversions

Most extensions will obviously change the roof line of a house to some extent, however some extensions involve <u>only</u> changes to the roof. Many houses and bungalows offer enormous potential for the conversion of roof space into additional rooms. Roof conversions can take many forms: utilising roof lights; dormer windows or even involve the creation of a complete new storey on top of an existing house.

The most successful roof conversions in planning terms are generally those which have the least visual impact. As with other sorts of extension there are a range of desirable and undesirable features which require consideration.

◆

Dormers

Rear facing dormer windows will usually be looked on more favourable than front facing ones. However, there is no reason why well designed dormers cannot make a house more attractive, so having them on the front need not necessarily be a problem. Generally speaking it is over-large, box-like dormer windows which will be frowned upon and they should be avoided.

- *Large box dormers like this look awful and destroy any attractive character a house might have. They would always be refused unless such box like front facing dormers are already a very common feature in an area. (New houses are sometimes built with them, but they would usually take the form of the one shown on page 54).*

Dormers should, in most cases, be physically small in proportion to the size of the roof as a whole. If they are very large and bulky they will detract from the character of a house. As a guide, the size of the dormer should represent less than half the distance between the ridge and eves of the main roof:

- *This drawing indicates a general principle, which although not rigid, usually results in an acceptably sized dormer. Namely that the depth of the dormer (a) should not exceed half the length of the roof slope (b). the dormer should also be below ridge level.*

The dormer will look more attractive if it reflects the pitch of the existing roof. The example below indicates the alien appearance of an over-large dormer which is out of keeping with the design of the house.

- *This dormer is too large and dominates the appearance of the building. Its proportions are entirely out of keeping with the style of the existing house.*

On many modern houses the size of the roof space will not allow a useable conversion into bedrooms without the addition of more space than a traditional dormer can provide. Large flat roofed dormers can be acceptable if they are constructed on the rear (or least public) elevation and do not make the house look top heavy. Although as always, if an area is characterised by flat roofed front facing dormers then it is likely that further such dormers would be approved.

- *This is an acceptable rear facing box dormer, acceptable because it has been carefully designed to sit within the roof slope. It is a minimum of one metre back from the eaves (i.e. the gutter) and its roof is below the ridge height of the house. It is also set back at least a 30 cm from the neighbouring house. Staining the wood boarding a dark colour would also make it less conspicuous.*

Converting a bungalow into a house

There are many bungalows which can satisfactorily be converted into two storey dwellings by the use of dormer windows or rooflights. Some bungalows however do not have adequate roof space to enable this to occur. Sometimes it is possible to convert a bungalow into a house by increasing the height of the roof in its entirety. It may then be necessary for dormers to be used, or it may involve the creation of a full additional storey.

- *This roof conversion employs dormers which give the house a "cottage" style appearance.*

Above and beyond the questions of detail and specific design issues one thing which needs to be established is: 'will there in principle be an objection to the conversion of a bungalow into a house?'

The answer to this question depends very much upon the character of the surrounding area and the physical relationship between the existing bungalow and its neighbours.

◆

The Character of the Area

In roads which have a mix of both houses and bungalows, or roads in which bungalows have been converted to two storeys, then the principle of a roof conversion or the addition of an upper storey is unlikely to be a problem, subject of course to the usual issues of good design and harm to neighbours.

In a residential area which contains nothing but bungalows, it is likely that a Planning Authority will be reluctant to permit the conversion of a bungalow into a full blown two storey house. This is because any such change would probably be considered 'out of character' with the area, and could lead to pressure for additional storeys on many bungalows. If a roof conversion can be carried out which keeps the ridge at the same height and uses dormer windows as described above, then this is in principle likely to be acceptable even in areas characterised by single storey houses.

It is wise to investigate the foundations of a bungalow to ensure that they are adequate for a roof conversion prior to spending money on planning.

◆

5.   Extensions to Houses in Open Countryside

Many of the factors which restrict the size of possible extensions to houses in towns and villages do not apply to houses situated in open countryside. Such houses may have few, if any, immediate neighbours. Problems of overlooking and overshadowing will therefore not apply and there may be no clearly identifiable 'character of the area' to come into conflict with.

This does not necessarily mean, however, that the maximum size of an extension will depend simply upon the amount of land available.

In areas of countryside which have special designations (see page 34) and to a lesser degree in open countryside as a whole, national and local planning policies tend to emphasise a restrictive approach to new development. The purpose of this is to protect the attractive appearance of rural areas.

As a consequence, it is not as easy to get planning permission to turn small cottages into large mansions as it once was.

Unless the Local Planning Authority indicate otherwise, it would be reasonable to expect to have to restrict extensions so that they remain in proportion with the existing house. Extensions which enlarge a house by in excess of 50% may be frowned upon, particularly in sensitive and prominent locations.

◆

6.   Outbuildings and Garages

If you need to apply for permission for outbuildings or a detached garage, then considerations of design will be as relevant as for other householder proposals. The design of free standing garages should relate to that of the house and be built of similar (or complimentary) materials. The illustration below indicates the importance of this when the existing house has an individual or particularly attractive character:

- *Double garages don't have to be boring boxes with no character. In this case following the design features of the main house works well.*

When the design of the house and its location is more mundane than the above example, then a more standard style of garage may be acceptable. Clearly the match of materials and design will not be as important to the appearance of a house as in the case of a physically linked extension. Nevertheless, the days of prefabricated concrete flat roofed garages are drawing to a close in many areas, except in the case of those garages built using permitted development rights. There is no need for all garages to be boring boxes. With a little extra expense and imagination they can be attractive and useful additions to a property. For example, having play rooms for kids above garages is becoming increasingly popular.

The siting of garages is important to the appearance of a street. The space needed for a garage with an area for turning and additional parking will be considerable. A minimum distance of 5.5m between garage doors and the highway will normally be required when a garage faces the road. As a consequence most garages are located or accessed down one side of the house. However, where there are garages situated forward of the house in a road, and front gardens are large, a garage in the front garden need not be an impossibility. In this case the amount of screening and planting available can have a significant effect upon the look of the proposal.

———————— ◆ ————————

7. Materials and Attention to Detail

The quality and choice of materials will be vital in achieving an attractive end result. There will normally be a condition attached to the planning permission which states that materials must match the existing materials to the satisfaction of the Planning Authority. Whether it is requested or not it is always advisable to submit a sample of the materials to be used to the Planning Department for their written confirmation that the materials are acceptable, ie a brick, tile or whatever, so that you are fully covered in the event of a dispute in the future.

The detailed features of a building are just as important as the overall scale and design. It will improve the appearance of any extension enormously if the detailed design reflects the details on the existing house - for instance where a particular brick bonding is used it should be copied. In older buildings decorative brickwork was often used, and other features such as interesting barge boards or chimneys may exist. If there are such features they should be echoed in the extension to help improve its appearance and integrate the new with the old.

———————— ◆ ————————

• *This one and a half storey side extension illustrates many of the design features which often enable additions to improve rather than detract from the appearance of an existing attractive house. A lower roof height; small well designed dormers; decorative brick details below the eve (gutter) line; a setting back of the new front wall from the existing, similar window styles and proportions to the original.*

The proportions and styles of doors and windows should match the existing house. This will be particularly important if the house is an older style building with some character. If an older style house (Victorian or earlier) has had original attractive sash windows removed, it may be a great opportunity to reinstate them. In my opinion aluminium or UPVC windows will always spoil the look of an old house. Incidentally, it is becoming apparent that some UPVC windows are less secure than wooden ones.

• *Dormers do not have to be pitched or flat roofed, this dormer is an attractive new feature on an already appealing house.*

- *Two front facing dormers which are well proportioned and small enough not to dominate the appearance of either house. They are therefore likely to be approved.*

- *Where a house has attractive original windows and brick details around the window openings, it is advisable to follow that design in an extension. Plastic windows cannot produce the same effect as the original wooden casement or sash windows shown above.*

- *The use of natural slate to match the existing roof and careful attention to the details of its design make this dormer an attractive addition.*

Where materials cannot be found which will be a reasonable match with the existing, then a completely different and contrasting material may be preferable. An example would be a rendered extension to a stone house. Provided that the colour of the render is appropriate this would be more visually pleasing than say artificial stone. The relevant Planning Department will be happy to assist in your choice.

◆

8.   Parking and Access

Planning authorities will as a matter of course consult the local highway authority regarding the effect of planning applications upon parking provision and road safety.

As a general rule all new houses and houses which are extended, will be required to have adequate on site parking spaces. The actual standards will differ throughout the country and be dependant to some extent upon the character of an area.

Usually houses with up to three bedrooms will need to have a minimum of two parking spaces. In some areas where on street parking is becoming a problem (such as tightly developed modern estates) additional spaces will be required for each bedroom added by way of an extension. This is based on the simple logic that the bigger the house the more potential there is for car ownership and traffic generation. Such standards follow research into traffic movements generated from houses and estates.

Parking standards may be flexible and it is worth requesting the relevant information from your local Planning Department at the earliest stage.

The loss of substantial areas of front garden to provide parking spaces is likely to be frowned upon by planners. This is despite the fact that you may turn your entire front garden into a hard standing without planning permission. However, remember that it is in the best interests of the appearance of the house and the street to retain as much greenery as possible.

———————— ◆ ————————

9. Hard Surfacing

The materials used to hard surface a driveway or parking area will have an important effect upon the whole appearance of your house. The use of good quality materials such as sets or paviours would be desirable, gravel can also be attractive. Concrete and tarmac are visually unappealing but the use of quality edging stones or curbs can make quite an improvement to the appearance of these more utilitarian surfaces.

———————— ◆ ————————

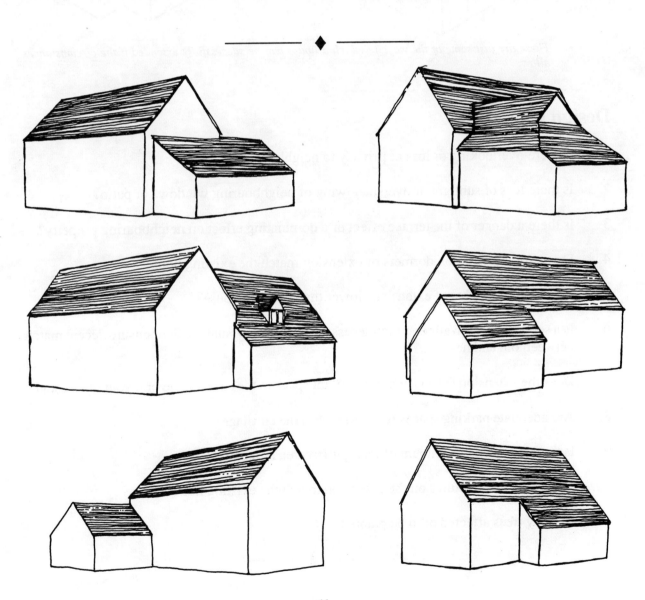

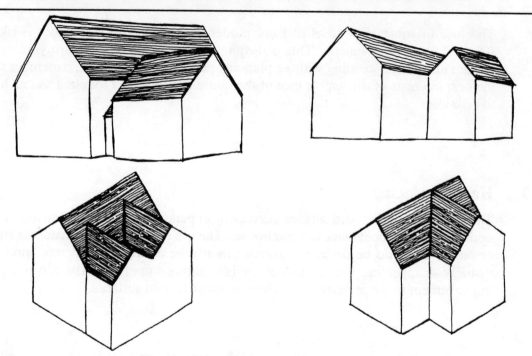

• *These are just some of the ways in which a house can be successfully extended if the circumstances allow.*

Design Checklist

1. Is there overlooking or loss of privacy to neighbours?

2. Is there loss of sunlight or overshadowing of neighbouring windows or patio?

3. Is there a danger of the terrace effect or a dominating effect on neighbouring property?

4. Do the roof pitches on dormers or extension match the existing house?

5. Are the roof heights of extensions lower than existing house?

6. Is a set back in the walls and roof necessary to create a visual break or ensure decent match between old and new?

7. Does the extension fill a visually important space in the street scene or layout of an estate?

8. Are adequate parking spaces retained within the curtilage?

9. Is there a reasonable amount of rear garden area remaining?

10. Do the detailed features on the extension match the existing house?

11. Are any trees affected or to be planted?

A House in your Garden?

Advice regarding the commercial development of land is beyond the scope of this guide, but I thought it useful to include this brief section on obtaining permission for a house in your garden. The 'infilling' of gaps between houses is a regular occurrence in most towns and villages and provides many homeowners with substantial windfalls, and many small builders with a regular income.

◆

The Options

If your house has a very large garden there are two options worth investigating, the building of a house or houses in addition to the existing house, or the demolition of the existing house and re-development of the whole plot.

◆

First Step

The creation of new building plots from existing garden land can take some imagination and experience. For those who are unfamiliar with such things it can be difficult to envisage building a house on what will often look like a small piece of land. Therefore my advice in the first instance is that you obtain a copy of the Ordnance Survey map of your vicinity from your local Planning Department (scale 1:1250).

◆

The Main Considerations

Having obtained this map you are in a good position to compare the size of your plot to the size and layout of houses in the area. You can compare the 'footprint' of houses in the vicinity to your piece of land and make a judgement as to whether you have enough land to create a building plot.

In addition to the physical size of the land available, a variety of other factors will need to be considered. To create a building plot the following requirements will usually need to be met:

* your existing house

    - must retain a reasonable rear garden, of at least $10^1/2$m in depth.

    - must have a minimum of two parking spaces (this includes any remaining garage etc) and a turning area (where situated on a main road)

    - must not be overlooked or overshadowed by the new house.

* the proposed new house

    – should have a plot with a reasonable width of road frontage, similar in size to the plots of other houses in the vicinity

    – should have a plot which is not significantly smaller than others in the vicinity

    – should have a reasonable private rear garden area

    – should have at least two parking spaces off the road, and a turning area, when access is onto a main road

    – should not overlook, overshadow or have an oppressive effect upon neighbouring houses

    – should have a safe access directly onto a road, rather than a new and indirect driveway running between existing houses. Utilising an existing access is desirable provided that it provides good visibility and the additional usage would not cause noise and disturbance to existing houses.

In general:

* 'Infill' development will only be allowed in towns and villages and tightly knit groups of houses, not in loose scatters of houses in open countryside.

* The development of garden land will not be allowed if it harms the character of an area, or will set a precedent for the intensification of housing in a spaciously developed neighbourhood.

* Infill development should not result in the loss of attractive trees, or trees protected by a Tree Preservation Order.

* In normal residential areas there is no reason why a 'bungalow' will be considered more favourably by the planners than a house, unless it is to avoid problems of overlooking etc.

* Many houses have narrow road frontages but long back gardens. The building of a house at the end of a garden, accessed by a drive running up the side of the existing house is not normally an acceptable form of housing layout.

* Applications for building plots in Conservation Areas or in the setting of Listed Buildings will be subject to particularly rigorous scrutiny by the Planning Department.

Remember, town planning does not necessarily mean 'town cramming'.

Building Plot Examples (see page 66)

Plot 1:   This large garden can be divided to create a building plot of the same size as the larger plots in the vicinity. There is a suitable road frontage and depth of rear garden and window to window distances will prevent any problem of overlooking.

Plot 2:   Sometimes described as 'backland' or 'tandem' development, this is not an acceptable way of creating a building plot. There is no road frontage and the access would cause noise and disturbance to the two houses on either side of it. The layout is entirely out of character with the surrounding area.

Plot 3:   This small house has a very large garden. This could be subdivided to make two or three additional plots, depending upon whether the existing house is demolished or not. Such a subdivision would create plots of a size and shape in keeping with the character of the surrounding area.

Plot 4:   This plot has been created by using land from three separate back gardens. A reasonable width of road frontage and depth of rear garden has been created. Windows on the proposed house would need to be positioned only on the front and back to avoid overlooking of the existing houses on either side. Unless a bungalow was built on the site.

Plot 5:   The small bungalow on this site has been demolished and replaced with a pair of semi-detached houses. Although the resulting plots are narrow they are not dissimilar to those directly opposite.

Plot 6:   This large side garden offers some potential on a building plot. However, there are houses close on three sides so overlooking and overshadowing could be a problem unless the proposed house is carefully designed and sited. A bungalow could be necessary to avoid problems.

———— ◆ ————

Building Plot Examples

Chapter 5

APPEALING AGAINST REFUSAL

Chapter 5
APPEALING AGAINST REFUSAL

You have had your application refused!

Reasons for Refusal

The decision notice has arrived and the reasons for refusal are given. The following examples are typical:

Conflict with character of existing dwelling

The proposed extension due to its design, bulk and siting fails to harmonise with the scale and character of the existing dwelling. The extension will appear as an intrusive incongruous feature to the substantial detriment of the character and amenities of the area.

Overlooking

The proposed development is poorly sited in that it would overlook and be overlooked by existing neighbouring property. Permission for such a development would have a detrimental effect on the character and amenities of that neighbouring property and the character and amenities of the development itself would be detrimentally affected by the neighbouring property.

Overshadowing

The scale, bulk and height of the proposed extension is excessive and would have an overshadowing and overbearing effect on neighbouring properties.

Reduction of existing rear garden

The proposal would result in an unacceptable reduction in the size of the existing rear garden, which would consequently be inadequate to serve the existing house.

Insufficient detail

This application cannot be considered acceptable without further details indicating the effects of the proposed development on the surrounding area, and despite a written request these details have not been submitted.

On the back of the decision notice or on a separate sheet will be the following address:

Secretary of State
Department of the Environment
Tollgate House
Houlton Street
Bristol
BS2 9DJ

This is the Department of the Environment office which will provide you with details of how to appeal and provide you with the relevant forms.

◆

What can be Appealed Against?

You may appeal if:

*   your application has been refused

*   you do not accept a condition which has been attached to a planning permission and wish to have it removed

*   if the Local Authority do not decide your application within eight weeks. This however is to be considered in the context of the time taken to determine the appeal. This eight week period appeal is usually used by people who, knowing they will be refused, wish to lodge an appeal as soon as possible (while perhaps negotiating on a duplicate application).

◆

Should you Appeal?

First - find out exactly what the problems are by talking directly to the Planning Officer involved. The reasons for refusal on the decision notice can sometimes be hard to follow! If you did not submit the proposal following consultations, find out if changes to the plans in a new application would overcome the reasons for refusal.

Second - find out from the Planning Department whether your application was considered by the Planning Committee. If it was, was it recommended for approval by the Planning Officers? If the committee overturned the advice of the Planning Officers then it may be that the issues were finely balanced or that the application was not refused for sound planning reasons. In this situation it is often worth appealing.

It is very difficult to talk in general terms about what is more or less likely to gain approval at appeal. The best guide is to consider what you applied for against the advice given in Chapter 4 of this book. If you live in an area which is designated as a Conservation Area, National Park or Area of Outstanding Natural Beauty then the level of restriction is going to be greater than outside these areas. Controls on the quality of materials, design, and emphasis on traditional local building styles will be greater. If you live in a normal, undistinguished residential area, then a refusal based purely on judgements about unattractive design is likely to be worth appealing against.

———— ◆ ————

Cost and Time

These are the two most influential factors in reaching the decision to go to appeal.

Cost – there is no fee to pay when making an appeal. The only costs are those resulting from paying for planning advice or representation, or the effort you may put in yourself.

You do not need to employ a professional planner to lodge an effective appeal. Provided you are clear about the arguments for and against your proposal and you feel confident, you should be able to make a reasonable case without outside help.

Time – this is often the Planning Officer's greatest bargaining point, although he or she is unlikely to mention this. Making an appeal is likely to take at least six months from start to finish, and could take up to a year. The type of appeal you choose will influence the length of time taken before a decision will be made.

———— ◆ ————

Who decides the outcome of a Planning Appeal?

Planning Appeals are decided by an Inspector appointed by and acting on behalf of the Secretary of State for the Environment at the Department of the Environment.

———— ◆ ————

What sort of Appeal should you make?

There are three sorts of appeal process:

1.   Written Representations
2.   Informal Hearings
3.   Public Inquiries

For most householder appeals, the first type is the most appropriate, although you may request any sort of appeal process. The Local Authority must agree with it, and in cases of dispute the Department of the Environment will decide. Either side can insist upon a Public Inquiry.

———— ◆ ————

1. **Written Representations**

    This is usually the easiest and quickest method of appeal.

    *   You make a written statement stating why you feel that you have a case, ie why permission should have been granted.

    *   The Local Authority will produce a written statement.

    *   You then exchange statements, and have an opportunity to comment on the other side's view.

    *   A Planning Inspector receives both statements, plus any additional factual background information and letters of objection or support from neighbouring residents or other interested parties.

    *   He or she will then make a site visit.

    *   You will be informed of the date and time of the site visit so that you can be present, but no discussion of the case is permitted on site.

    *   After due consideration, the Inspector informs both parties of his or her decision by letter.

    *   Any interested party may request from the Inspector that he/she is also sent a copy.

    ◆

2. **Informal Hearings**

    *   The hearing consists of a meeting between yourself (with or without an agent), a representative of the local Planning Department, a Planning Inspector and any other interested parties such as neighbours.

    *   The pros and cons of the proposal will then be discussed. In this method written statements are exchanged before the hearing, but you are entitled to see the Local Authority's before you submit your own.

    *   A site visit will be made, and the Inspector may continue discussions at the site.

    *   The Inspector will then go away, consider what he has heard and inform both parties by letter of his decision.

    ◆

3.   **Public Inquiries**

*   The public inquiry procedure is very formal and can be quite intimidating to the uninitiated. It is usual for both sides to be represented by solicitors or barristers or other advocates.

*   Statements of case are read by planning witnesses and each side has the opportunity of cross examining the other and of making a final verbal summing up.

*   Public inquiries are usually reserved for significant development proposals or complicated cases involving unauthorised developments.

———— ♦ ————

Which sort of appeal is best?

The choice for the householder involved in small scale proposals (including such things as single building plot proposals) is between written representation or informal hearings.   Written representations are the quickest (if quick is the word!) although if you feel you are better at explaining your case verbally rather than in writing the informal hearing may be more attractive. It is reassuring to note that Planning Inspectors are trained to take account of the difficulties faced by householders attempting to justify their proposals against experienced planners. This being the case, an informal hearing may often be worth trying if time is not of the essence. Anyone may be present at such a hearing including supporters and objectors to your scheme.

———— ♦ ————

Who can Appeal?

The only person who can appeal against a refusal of permission is the person who made the planning application. There is no right of appeal by objectors to an application who feel that it should not have been permitted, nor can an appeal be made by someone in support of a planning application which has been refused. Anyone can appeal against a condition which they want to remove from the planning permission.

———— ♦ ————

What do you say?

Arguments in favour of your proposal should be confined to those aspects which are relevant to planning - these things are called 'material considerations'.

The following factors are not generally considered 'material' to the determination of an appeal so there is no point in putting these forward in your case.

* your property would be more valuable

* the proposal would improve your view

* you need the extra space

* there has been a lot of development in the area recently anyway

* your intentions are not based on financial gain

* you have been able to get a cheap deal on the design and materials proposed

* you are a local person.

Factors which are more likely to be material considerations and which could be worth mentioning if they apply, are:

* The harmless effect of the proposal on the residential amenities of neighbouring houses, in terms of:

    − privacy
    − sunlight and daylight
    − aspect

* The effect of the proposal in terms of its appearance and the visual amenities of its surroundings. Arguments in favour of the look of the proposal may include:

    − The proposal <u>is</u> in keeping with its surrounds. <u>Either</u> because the design and siting and general scale reflect those elements found in other buildings in the area, <u>or</u> the surroundings have no special or discernible 'character' or particular features with which it is necessary or desirable to conform.

    − The Local Authority have not in their policies identified the area, which includes the application site, as having any special character or significance, or as containing any special features worthy of preservation. Therefore a refusal in terms of design alone is unjustified.

    − The proposal is similar in appearance to other extensions (etc) permitted elsewhere in the vicinity.

    − Entirely suitable materials are being proposed for use in the development if it is approved.

    − No trees are being affected, new trees and shrubs will be planted.

* More general arguments might include:

    − The views from neighbouring properties are not relevant, there is no right to a certain view.

- The application should be considered on its merits and only be refused if there is "demonstrable harm to interests of acknowledged importance" – planning jargon for a very good reason!

- Although the application does not conform with some elements of the Development Plan, other material considerations indicate that it should be approved.

* Planning Policies

It may be worth glancing at the relevant local "Development Plan" for any arguments which would support your case, or indications that you might as well give up and negotiate, or abandon the proposal altogether.

◆

Local Plans

A Local Plan is a document which contains planning policies for the area covered by a particular Local Planning Authority. It is produced after a long process of public consultation and is agreed by the Department of the Environment. Such Plans tend to be revised every five years. The policies contained in them tend to be most influential when the Plan is up to date and has been formally adopted by the Council concerned. The older a Local Plan is the less 'weight' an Appeal Inspector will give it when balancing the pros and cons of a proposal. Local Plans often contain policies which are relevant to small scale private developments such as house extensions.

A planning application will normally be determined in accordance with the policies contained in the relevant Local Plan. The exception to this is when that Local Plan is clearly out of date or when there are special circumstances related to a particular proposal.

◆

Structure Plans

These relate to whole Counties rather than to Districts or Boroughs. They set out general planning principles for an area and overall goals which need to be met (for instance the total number of houses to be permitted). These Plans are unlikely to affect domestic applications.

◆

Government Advice

This is contained primarily in Planning Policy Guidance Notes issued by the Department of the Environment. These PPG's cover the whole range of planning issues and are updated on a fairly regular basis. This Government advice is important but it is only one of the influences which the Inspector will weight up when deciding the merits of a particular case.

The Inspector is likely to be very familiar with this advice and will not need reminding of it.

The majority of homeowner planning applications will not be determined one way or another due to specific planning policies. For those that are, these policies are likely to be contained in the relevant Local Plan. Therefore, when making an Appeal it may be worth examining a copy at your local Planning Department and seeking advice as to what parts, if any, are relevant in your case.

--------- ◆ ---------

Will the Planning Department help you to Appeal?

You have the right to see public documents relating to your application and details of other planning permissions etc held by your local Planning Department. Before appealing it would be worth investigating the history of planning decisions related to your house, and perhaps similar proposals in the area. Odd though it sounds, the Planning Department still have the job of assisting you, even if it is to appeal against their refusal! Therefore do not be afraid to seek the advice of Planning Officers when making an appeal, even if you know they do not support your proposal.

--------- ◆ ---------

What if you Lose the Appeal?

The Inspector's decision letter will clearly set out the reasons for the decision. It may be that you can overcome these problems by changes to your proposal - e.g. by removing an overlooking window or reducing the height of a roof. In that case, submit a new application accordingly.

You can only challenge the decision on a point of law, or if you feel that the requirements of planning legislation or procedures have been ignored. You cannot challenge it simply because you disagree with the decision. Any challenge has to made through the High Court, and expensive legal advice will be needed. My advice is to forget it.

--------- ◆ ---------

'Unreasonable' Decisions

Local Planning Departments try, with varying degrees of success and with varying degrees of effort, to impose their notion of good design upon developments within their area. This includes house extensions. The ultimate test of how 'reasonable' these Planning Departments are being is whether their decisions are upheld by the Secretary of State's Inspectors if someone appeals against a refusal. In some cases Planning Authorities will insist upon changes to design, or will refuse extensions, which would receive permission from a Planning Inspector at appeal. This is unfortunately a fact of life. Such 'unreasonable' demands by planning authorities are perhaps made more possible with householder extensions than with other planning applications because large numbers of people do not have the time or inclination to go to appeal. Ultimately if you do not like what a Planning Department requests or demands, a planning appeal to the Secretary of State is your only option. At Public Inquiries and Informal Hearings 'costs' may be awarded against <u>either side</u> if it is demonstrated that one or other has acted 'unreasonably'. This is not easy to prove and is not relevant for most householder applications, as costs cannot yet be awarded in written appeals.

The Ombudsman

If you feel strongly that you have been seriously disadvantaged because the Planning Authority has not followed the correct <u>procedure</u> in dealing with an application, then you can make a complaint to the Ombudsman. You can complain if you are the applicant, neighbour, or anyone else. However it is very important to understand that the Ombudsman is not interested in the professional judgement of the planners, he is there purely to police the correct implementation of administrative procedures. Remember also that if you think certain procedures should have been carried out make sure that you thoroughly understand what should have been done, and be clear about exactly what omission you object to, and why.

More information regarding the work of the Ombudsman may be obtained from:

The Secretary
Commission for Local Administration in England
21 Queen Anne's Gate
London
SW1H 9BU.

Conclusion

Don't be afraid to appeal if you were advised initially by the Planning Officers that your proposal appeared acceptable. Do not be afraid to seek advice regarding the appeal from the Planning Department.

Chapter 6

HOW TO OBJECT TO SOMEONE ELSE'S PLANNING APPLICATION

Chapter 6
HOW TO OBJECT TO SOMEONE ELSE'S PLANNING APPLICATION

Why Bother?

There are essentially three reasons why it is useful to object to an application with which you disagree.

1. You may draw attention to problems caused by the proposal which the Planning Officers may otherwise overlook.

2. In a borderline case, when the proposal is considered just acceptable, your objection could swing the balance in favour of refusal.

3. You may influence the elected Councillors, who may consequently refuse the application.

―――――――――― ◆ ――――――――――

Finding out about the Application

In some Districts you will be personally notified by card or letter about an application made by one of your neighbours. In other Districts the application may be advertised by means of a notice (usually orange) pinned up on the site for a minimum of twenty-one days. In all areas a list of planning applications will be placed regularly in one or more local papers. If you hear about it on the grapevine, telephone the Planning Department to confirm it. In all cases it is worth visiting the Planning Department or Parish or Town Council to look at the plans. Do not rely upon plans shown to you by the applicant. If you are unclear what is intended, get advice from a Planning Officer. Make sure you find out the last date for objections to be received. This will usually be, in practice, the day before the relevant Planning Committee. If the proposal can be determined by the Chief Planning Officer then he/she will be at liberty to make that decision after about three weeks from the applications date of registration. Planning Authorities are legally obliged to inform any objectors to a proposal, about the outcome of the planning application.

―――――――――― ◆ ――――――――――

How do you Object?

Applicants generally seem to be far more offended by objectors who complain immediately to the Council than by those who approach them in person. It is therefore sensible, in the first instance, to talk directly to the applicant and diplomatically explain your concerns. This might not change anything but it could avoid a neighbourhood feud! When objecting to the Council always object in writing, and quote the application number. Talk to your local Councillor and explain your concerns; provide them with a copy of your letter. In some parts of the country, objectors are allowed to speak directly to the Planning Committee. In other areas objectors may address a small premeeting to express their concerns. In most cases objections can only be made in writing and verbally to Planning Officers or Councillors during the weeks prior to the committee.

Groups of protestors sometimes get together and organise a petition against a particular proposal. In my view such lists of signatures are fairly easy to collect in large numbers and are not nearly as effective as individual letters of objection.

———————— ◆ ————————

What do you say?

It is best to confine your comments to those which are relevant to planning - these things are called material considerations. If you do include objections which are not relevant in planning terms they will be ignored, but they may direct attention away from your objections which are relevant and should be noticed.

The following are not generally considered 'material' to the determination of an application, so you would (usually) be wasting effort complaining about them:

*   a fall in the value of your property

*   the loss of an attractive view from your particular house

*   your speculations - e.g. 'this might be the thin end of the wedge'

*   a lot of recent development in your area

*   commercial harm from additional competition to your business

*   that the development was initially done without permission

*   personal dislike or suspicion of the applicant or his intentions.

In contrast, the most relevant considerations in planning terms (therefore the ones which you should use) include:

*   the physical impact of the proposal in terms of:

     –   loss of privacy

     –   loss of sunlight

     –   the effect on the immediate view from your windows

     –   dominating and oppressive effect over your house or garden.

* the physical effects in more general terms such as:

    – design out of character with the surrounding area

    – creation of a damaging precedent which would encourage similar applications elsewhere which would individually and collectively harm the area

    – similarity with previous applications which were refused (either on the same property or elsewhere)

    – loss of or damage to attractive trees

    – poor materials

    – excessive height in comparison with other buildings in the area

    – loss of important views into open countryside (when part of the village or town's character)

    – loss of attractive green spaces within built up areas

    – creation of an excessively high density development out of character with the surrounding area.

* Planning policies. These are contained in government documents and plans produced by County Councils and District Councils. These may be relevant to the range of small scale domestic developments considered by this guide, but the planners know about them anyway.

———— ◆ ————

How do you say it?

When writing a letter of objection begin the letter by quoting the Planning Application Number, the relevant address and description of the proposal.

* Consider carefully what you intend to say.

* Don't ramble and include irrelevant information.

* Don't be emotional and make personal comments about the applicant.

* Don't exaggerate, be honest and realistic.

* Set out the reasons for your objections one by one and follow each with brief details.

* Type the letter.

———— ◆ ————

Conclusion

Planning approval is not dependent upon a lack of objections, nor will it necessarily be withheld if objections are made. Objections can be useful in drawing attention to problems which have been overlooked, and influencing the elected Councillors one way or the other. It is important to remember that if you wish to raise objections, be polite, don't be aggressive or personal, or your comments may be counter productive.

♦

Chapter 7

HOW UNAUTHORISED DEVELOPMENT IS CONTROLLED

Chapter 7
HOW UNAUTHORISED DEVELOPMENT IS CONTROLLED

Many people are unclear about the requirements of planning permission and despite having the best of intentions they can find themselves at odds with the Local Planning Department. This can occur because of simple ignorance, incorrect advice or a lack of communication between the different parties involved in a development. If you are in this position, don't panic. Planning Authorities frequently have to deal with such occurances and if the situation is approached the right way it can usually be resolved amicably and without drama.

In some cases people intentionally seek to undermine and ignore planning controls for their own ends. In these circumstances effective legal action can be taken.

---◆---

Enforcement

'Enforcement' is a Local Authority's term for the set of procedures used to enforce planning laws. Planning Departments usually have 'enforcement officers' who spend their time following up complaints about unauthorised development. The legal procedures and ins and outs of the enforcement system are complicated and beyond the scope of this guide, but a summary is outlined below to help those who have become involved. This includes those people who believe that others seem to have 'got away with it'. Recently new legislation has strengthened the planners' powers in this area.

---◆---

Safe After Four Years

It is not an offence to build something without planning permission. If something has been built without permission for four years and no action has been taken by the Planning Authority during that time, then the unauthorised building becomes immune from enforcement. This is known as the four year rule. The logic behind this must be that if something can go unnoticed for four years it can't be much of a problem, so it effectively gets permission! The four year rule also applies to the change of use of any building into a dwelling, but not to other changes of use, which fall under the ten year rule.

The ten year rule applies to conditions attached to a planning permission. If they have not been complied with within ten years, then in most cases they cannot be enforced.

---◆---

Will Enforcement Action Always be Taken?

Local Authorities are acting within their powers <u>not</u> to take enforcement action if they feel that the time and expense involved would not be justified. The fact that something has been done without permission is not by itself a good enough reason for a Planning Department to object to it, although they will be justified in seeking to legitimise it by requesting the submission of a retrospective planning application.

There are basically three situations in which enforcement may be needed:

*   When something has been built, or an activity is occurring, which requires, but does not have, planning permission.

*   When planning permission has been granted for something but it is not being (or has not been) built in accordance with the plans submitted.

*   When permission has been granted subject to conditions but these have been ignored.

The following procedures are likely to be adopted by the enforcement officer in dealing with the first two possibilities.

———— ◆ ————

Negotiation and Request for Retrospective Application

An enforcement officer working with the Planning Department will investigate the breach and make a visit to the property involved. If it is considered that what has occurred is likely to be acceptable or made acceptable through minor changes then negotiations may be attempted. As part of these negotiations a retrospective planning application may be requested. A time limit is likely to be given by the Planning Authority to the person responsible to either rectify the breach or make an application.

———— ◆ ————

Requests for Further Information

Legal steps can be taken to find out more about the breach of control:

*   Requisition for Information Notice - This is served in order to establish who has a legal interest in the property involved.

*   Planning Contravention Notice - In addition to the above questions this notice can ask for specific and detailed information about the nature of the breach.

In both cases failure to complete and return the relevant forms, or the giving of false information can result in the prosecution of the person responsible.

———— ◆ ————

Enforcement Notice

This is the main tool used by Planning Authorities against unauthorised developments and other breaches of planning control.

The Enforcement Notice is a legal notice served upon the person involved in the breach of planning control if:

* A Retrospective Planning Application is not submitted.

* A Retrospective Application is submitted but is subsequently refused.

* The breach is considered unacceptable and undesirable irrespective of the submission of an Application.

The Enforcement Notice outlines the nature of the breach of planning control and the steps required to rectify it and why it should be rectified. The Notice will 'take effect' a minimum of one month after it is served. If an appeal is not lodged at least one month after it takes effect then the person involved may be prosecuted and fined on a regular basis until the breach has been rectified (e.g. the unauthorised building is demolished).

Appealing against the Enforcement Notice

An appeal against the Enforcement Notice may be made to the Department of the Environment within one month of the Notice taking effect. The appeal will follow basically the same course as a normal Planning Appeal (see Chapter 5). If the appellant wins the appeal then they have got planning permission, this may be subject to conditions. If the appeal is lost and the breach is not rectified during the time given by the Appeal Inspector then prosecution can take place.

Stop Notices

A Stop Notice is available which can be served immediately following an Enforcement Notice. This may be required when some unauthorised activity is taking place which is harmful, e.g. ongoing building works or unpleasant industrial activities. The stop notice means that whatever is going on must cease, or prosecution will result immediately. These notices are not served often because if someone appeals against a Stop Notice and it transpires that the Notice was legally incorrect, then the Local Planning Authority could be liable to pay compensation for any lost income resulting from the Notice.

Time

The above courses of action obviously can take a considerable length of time, particularly if the person responsible for the unauthorised building or other activity appeals. They may appeal against the refusal of a planning application, and having lost that, appeal again against the subsequent Enforcement Notices and still lose. The process can take perhaps two years, during which local people may think nothing is being done. The long winded procedure also means that unauthorised business activities may continue to cause considerable inconvenience and disturbance to neighbouring residents, whilst the legal procedures are followed. Sensible Planning Authorities will serve an Enforcement Notice upon the refusal of a retrospective application to speed up the process and have both appeals considered at once.

———— ◆ ————

Enforcement of Conditions

In the event of people failing to implement planning conditions, the Local Authority may take immediate and effective action.

For example, if one of the conditions of your permission notice is that a certain window must be obscure glazed (to prevent overlooking) and this has not been done, a Breach of Condition Notice may be served upon you which will demand that the obscure glazing is done. A minimum of 28 days will be given by the notice for the work to be carried out. If this is not done, magistrates may impose a fine for every day until the condition has been complied with. The only defence in court against prosecution is that the person charged took all reasonable measures to carry out what is required by the notice, i.e. there had to be a jolly good reason why it has not been done!

This is a speedy and effective means of enforcement which could prove expensive for the person charged, and give them a criminal record. Conditions may be appealed against at any time (see page 68) but to carry out a development without complying risks prosecution, whether an appeal has been lodged or not.

———— ◆ ————

Amended Plans

Once planning permission has been granted applicants sometimes change their minds about certain aspects of a proposal, or find that it cannot physically be built in the form originally intended. This results in a request to amend the original plans. Although there is no legal procedure for accepting minor changes to approved schemes, Local Authorities will usually accept them if the original proposal was not controversial. In this context 'minor' means small in comparison to the overall proposal, for example to change the position of an extension by a couple of metres or raise or lower the roof a metre or so, or re-position windows etc. It is essential to agree amendments with the planners before building them in case they are not acceptable, and to avoid accusations that you are ignoring the system.

———— ◆ ————

Conclusion - The Right Attitude

As a general rule Local Planning Authorities do not have the manpower to check that all new buildings that are built have planning permission, or that they are built in exact accordance with the plans granted planning permission. Therefore enforcement action is likely to be the result of complaints from neighbours or the vigilance of local Parish or Town Councils.

Planning Authorities do not go around looking for trouble, and they are advised by Central Government to seek compromise in dealing with unauthorised development. On the other hand, the planning system exists to control development in the public interest and people do not like seeing it ignored.

So whatever the problem encountered, taking the right attitude will help. Whether you are an objector, or someone who has built something without permission, talking to the planners in a civil and helpful manner is more likely to achieve what you want than being difficult.

Note: Unauthorised works to Listed Buildings are not considered in this Chapter and may be dealt with by immediate prosecution and severe penalties.

———— ◆ ————

Chapter 8

TREES

Chapter 8
TREES

Planners as you might imagine are keen on trees. They add a great deal of beauty in town, villages and the countryside.

Trees may be protected in three ways:

1.   by a Tree Preservation Order (TPO)

2.   by being located in a Conservation Area

3.   by a planning condition.

Each situation is considered below.

——————— ◆ ———————

1.   **Tree Preservation Orders**

Councils may protect trees they consider of value by serving a Tree Preservation Order. This may be served on anything from individual trees in private gardens to extensive woodlands. Trees under the protection of a TPO can only be pruned or felled with the Council's consent. The exceptions to this are when:

*   the tree is dead, dying or dangerous

*   the tree has to be cut down or pruned in connection with the work of a statutory body, such as the electricity board or water authority

*   the tree has to be removed as part of a development which has been granted planning permission by the Council. This is assuming that the tree's removal is specifically mentioned as part of that approved scheme.

A TPO allows the Council's tree experts to make sure that proposals to prune a tree are necessary and will not harm its health or appearance. A tree not subject to a TPO, which is threatened with felling or unsuitable pruning, may be preserved as a matter of urgency by including it in a provisional TPO. This remains effective for up to six months while the Council considers whether to confirm it.

If a tree subject to an Order is removed, deliberately killed or damaged, the Planning Authority can prosecute the person carrying out the work, who may then be fined and required to replace the tree at their own expense. In certain circumstances the removal of a preserved tree may be agreed, but the owner will usually be required to replace the tree with one of a suitable species and size.

Some trees cannot be the subject of a TPO. For example:

* trees standing on Crown land (unless a Government Department agrees to the order)

* fruit trees grown for their fruit, either in orchards or private gardens.

A TPO has to be served on everyone who has a legal interest in the land involved. Any of these people have a right of appeal to the Council against the inclusion of trees in an order.

Details of TPOs within your area can be obtained from the Planning Department. Applications for the felling or pruning of protected trees should be in the form of a letter stating the location and species of tree, and the type of work proposed. No fee is required.

2.   **Trees in Conservation Areas**

All trees in Conservation Areas are subject to additional protection. Those not already included in a TPO may only be pruned or felled after the Council has been given six weeks written notice of the proposed work. This period allows the Council to assess the tree's visual importance and to make a TPO if necessary.

3.   **Planning Conditions**

When these exist on the site of a proposal, then conditions will often be attached to ensure that the trees are protected during construction works and are not removed. Quite often conditions will be used to ensure the planting of additional trees on a site. Planning conditions are useful in planting, maintaining and protecting trees in the short term but they do not offer real long term protection in the same way as a TPO.

Trees and your Planning Application

The presence of large trees in your garden can have a significant impact upon your ability to extend etc. The complication with trees is their effect upon the light available to windows, the effect of their roots on foundations and the effect of damage to their roots - all of which can have potentially serious consequences. The types of trees available and how to protect and deal with existing trees is beyond the scope of this guide. Either talk to the local Council's tree officer (if they have one) or employ a qualified arboriculturalist.

If trees are attractive and visually important in an area, then it is quite possible that permission for extensions etc will be refused in order to prevent their loss.

Points to remember:

*   Always check before felling or making substantial surgery on a mature tree that it is not the subject of a TPO. If it is, then you could face substantial fines unless you obtain the consent of your Local Authority.

*   A TPO is overridden by a planning application where the removal of the tree is specified.

*   Many trees, although not under a TPO, may be protected by conditions attached to previous planning permissions.

Trees & Building Works

*   Trees should be carefully protected during building works, avoid the storage of building materials or top soil under trees.

*   No machinery, particularly cement mixers, should be placed under trees. No vehicles should be parked or driven under trees as this causes damaging soil compaction.

*   Rising or lowering soil levels under the branch spread of trees can cause serious damage to their health.

*   Wherever possible all building works and ground disturbance should be done **outside** the branch spread of trees.

*   There are special kinds of foundations available which can accommodate existing roots without harm to the tree or damage to the house in the future.

*   Avoid cutting any tree roots larger than two inches in diameter.

N.B. Tree pruning should be done by experts, according to British Standard 3998 (1066). Incorrect cutting is likely to cause damage and decay. Never resort to lopping - the cutting of branches without regard to the appearance of the crown spread of the tree.

Chapter 9

BUILDING CONSENT AND REGULATIONS

Chapter 9
BUILDING CONSENT AND REGULATIONS

Building Regulations Approval is an entirely separate requirement to planning permission. This brief chapter is included because once planning permission is obtained you will usually need to get Building Regulations Consent. However, there are a range of building works which require Building Regulations Approval but not planning permission, and vice versa. Sometimes you don't need either.

A Building Regulations application can be made to your Local Authority or to the National House Builders Federation or to any other organisation approved by the Government for that purpose. This chapter has been written on the basis that you will be seeking approval from your Local Authority, (although this does not indicate any recommendation one way or another).

Is Building Regulation Approval Required?

Firstly, the building works that **DO** require approval:

1. Extensions (other than a porch or conservatory - see next section points 3 and 4).

2. Loft conversions.

3. Internal alterations, if they are of a structural nature and involve load bearing walls, joists, lintels, beams or chimney breasts (if in any doubt seek professional advice).

4. Conversion of a house into flats.

5. To create a new bathroom, where the work involves new drainage or plumbing.

6. To install or alter a heating appliance or system:

    (a) using gas, unless the work is supervised by British Gas

    (b) solid fuel

    (c) oil.

7. Cavity wall insulation. If you use an approved installer they will generally submit a building notice as part of the job.

8. Underpinning of foundations or floors. This is a structural alteration.

9. To convert your garage into a habitable room.

The building works which **DO NOT** require approval:

1. Carports. Provided they are less than 30m^2 in floor area and open on at least 2 sides.

2. Covered yards or covered ways to the house. Provided that the floor area is less than 30m^2.

3. Porches. Provided that the floor area is less than 30m^2, the existing front door is retained and a WC is not included.

4. Conservatories. Provided that they are built at ground floor level, the floor area is less than 30m^2 and the roof is glazed with transparent or translucent materials.

5. Detached buildings in the garden (including garages, greenhouses and sheds). Provided that they are each less than 30m^2 in floor area, do not provide sleeping accommodation and are either positioned at least one metre from the boundary or are single storey and constructed wholly of non-combustible material.

6. New windows. Provided that window openings are not enlarged as this would be a structural alteration to the house.

7. General repairs. Provided that they do not in any way affect the structure of the building. Repairs may include replacing the felt to a flat roof, re-tiling a roof provided that the new tiles are of the same type. If in any doubt consult a professional, or the Council's Building Inspector.

8. New bathroom fittings (see point 5 in previous section).

9. Construction of a boundary wall.

If you wish to confirm any of the above, or require clarification on any points, don't hesitate to ask the building regulations department of your local Council, that is why they are there.

———— ◆ ————

Making a Building Regulations Application

When seeking approval from your local Council there are two alternative methods which you may use:

1. **The Deposit of Full Plans**

    In this method you or your agent submits to the Council duplicate application forms with two full sets of drawings of the work you propose. These drawings must be sufficiently detailed to enable the Council to determine whether the work will comply with the relevant regulations, and should include:

    *   a site plan at a scale of 1:1250 clearly showing the proposed building or extension and with a clear indication of the boundaries of the property

* plans, sections and elevations as necessary to a scale of 1:50 or 1:100

* detailed specifications of all materials and methods of construction used

* appropriate calculations of thermal insulation and structural elements where reliance is not placed on the information contained in the approved documents attached to the regulations.

If the information submitted is deficient or inadequate it will delay the application and may result in a rejection of the plans. However, most Councils will contact you to seek clarification of what you propose, or amendments, when this would lead to an approval.

When such an application is approved you or your agent receives:

* a notice of approval
* a set of drawings stamped as approved
* printed inspection request cards.

These documents are usually necessary should you be seeking finance to assist in the extension or building work from a bank or building society and are useful on sale of the house to show that the necessary approvals were obtained. The approval notice and approved plans are important documents, they cannot normally be replaced, and should be kept safely, as should all written correspondence from the Council.

———— ◆ ————

2. **The Building Notice Procedure**

This method is somewhat easier and simpler, initially, than the deposit of full plans. You or your agent simply make a written application on the appropriate form and may start work straight away. (Subject to any necessary planning permission or the receipt of any relevant Home Improvement Grant). Full plans are not required, although a 1:1250 block plan with boundaries and any new buildings or extensions clearly marked is usually necessary. The control of building work is exercised by site inspection at the necessary stages.

On receipt of a valid notice in this form your local Council will respond with:

* a document accepting the building notice
* printed inspection request cards.

You do not receive written approval of your proposals.

During the progress of the work you may be asked to provide details and calculations of particular elements of your work, but you will not be asked for full plans. Plans requested in this case must be 'necessary' for the Council to determine compliance and will be requested in writing.

Obviously, to follow this method the builders must be capable of undertaking the work without drawings. The object of the Building Control Officer in making inspections is not to supervise the operation. The Building Control Officer will not act as a design consultant or surveyor on your behalf. There are disadvantages to such a method and you should carefully consider them before embarking upon building work by building notice.

Generally speaking I would only advise using this method for very small scale building works. If work to be approved under the notice system is sub-standard, then it will have to be taken down and re-built. The builder responsible may attempt to pass the cost on to you, at the very least it will cause hassle and waste time. Where the work involves building over a public sewer then it would be very foolhardy to proceed without the security of a full plans approval, as the water authority can require that the building or extension be removed.

Building Regulation Fees

Building regulation fees are set by Government statute and are payable in two stages. A plans fee must be paid upon deposit of full plans, and is intended to cover some of the costs of the Council in processing and approving the application.

A further fee (which is known as the inspection fee) is payable once the work starts on site .

Where a building notice is used the building notice fee (which is in fact the sum of the plans fee and the inspection fee payable for a full plans submission) is collected by invoice in the same way as an inspection fee. Details of the levels of fees are available from your Council offices.

Do Neighbours Have the Right to Object?

No. However, it is always advisable to be neighbourly and to tell them what you are doing. You may find that it could help to have access from their land in the future. Remember that you should not build on or over their land without their formal written consent.

Can you Appeal?

Yes. If you consider that rejection is not justified or you wish to have a particular requirement relaxed, you may appeal to the Secretary of State for the Environment within one month of the Local Authority's refusal.

What Happens if Your Work Does Not Comply?

The Local Authority can serve a notice on you to alter or remove it.

◆

Are There Penalties for Contravening Building Regulations?

Yes. If you build without notifying the Local Authority, or carry out work which does not comply then you are liable to be fined. The penalty may be up to £2000, plus £50 for each day the contravention continues after conviction. However, it is my understanding that once a building is fully completed for 12 months or more it is extremely difficult for a Local Authority to prosecute you. Remember, legal proceedings may be taken against you, and your builder.

◆

Information on Building Standards

Guidance may be obtained from:

* The Building Act 1984

* The Building Regulations 1991 (as amended)

* Approved HMSO documents (practical guidance about some of the ways of meeting the requirements of the regulations)

* British Standards

* British Board of Agreement Certificates

* Building Research Establishment

* Timber Research and Development Association.

These books will often be available at public libraries. You are not obliged to use any particular solution to meet the structural requirements of the regulations other than when providing a means of escape for fire purposes. However, if you do not follow the guidance in the approved documents you will have to be prepared to demonstrate that the requirements have been met. If in any doubt obtain professional advice.

◆

MODEL APPLICATIONS

COURTLAND DISTRICT COUNCIL
HOUSEHOLDER PLANNING APPLICATION
APPLICATION FOR PERMISSION TO CARRY OUT DEVELOPMENT - TOWN AND COUNTRY PLANNING ACTS.
THIS FORM IS ONLY TO BE USED FOR APPLICATIONS FOR EXTENSIONS TO HOUSES AND OTHER
DEVELOPMENT WITHIN THE CURTILAGE OF SINGLE RESIDENTIAL DWELLINGS.

Please answer ALL QUESTIONS in BLOCK LETTERS. If a question is not applicable, answer N/A in space. Please send FOUR copies of this form and plans to:

FOR OFFICE USE ONLY

THE DIRECTOR OF PLANNING SERVICES,
COURTLAND DISTRICT COUNCIL,
COUNCIL OFFICES, COURT STREET,
COURTLAND, BERKSHIRE

1.		APPLICANT'S NAME	MR & MRS. A. PLICANT
		ADDRESS	2 MEADOWSIDE COTTAGES. MEADOWSIDE ROAD. COURTLAND
		POSTCODE	CT4 5JG PHONE
2.	If the applicant has an agent, all correspondence will be sent to the agent.	AGENT'S NAME	MR. A. GENT
		ADDRESS	THE STUDIO. FAIRFIELD ROAD. COURTLAND. CT5 9PQ
		CONTACT NAME	MR. A. GENT PHONE (0441) 61249
3.	Show the site outline in RED on the plans	SITE ADDRESS OR LOCATION	2 MEADOWSIDE COTTAGES MEADOWSIDE ROAD. COURTLAND.
4.	WHAT IS THE APPLICATION FOR? Give brief details, including whether proposal is for single storey or two storey construction.	PROPOSAL	TWO STOREY SIDE EXTENSION. SINGLE STOREY REAR EXTENSION.
5.	LIST ALL PLANS AND DRAWINGS SUBMITTED WITH THIS APPLICATION		LOCATION PLAN 1/2500 , SITE PLAN 1/500 FLOOR PLANS 1/100 , ELEVATIONS 1/100.
6.	WILL THE PROPOSED EXTERNAL MATERIALS (WALLS AND ROOF) MATCH THE EXISTING?	YES/NO	If no, give details of materials to be used.
7.	IS THE SITE BOUNDARY TO BE ALTERED?	YES/NO	If yes, give details on the plans.
8.	(a) WILL SURFACE WATER DRAINAGE BE ALTERED?	YES/NO	If yes, give details on the plans.
	(b) WILL FOUL WATER DRAINAGE BE ALTERED?	YES/NO	If yes, give details on the plans.
9.	ARE ANY TREES TO BE FELLED?	YES/NO	If yes, give details on the plans.
10.	WILL ANY PEDESTRIAN OR VEHICULAR ACCESS BE ALTERED?	YES/NO	If yes, give details on the plans.
11.	IS FEE ENCLOSED?	YES/NO	If no, give reasons why.

I hereby apply for permission in respect of the particulars described above and in the attached plans and drawings. If planning permission is granted, the development must be carried out strictly in accordance with the approved plans. Failure to do so could result in enforcement action being taken. Permission under the Town & Country Planning Acts does not obviate the possible need to apply for Building Regulations Approval or any other necessary Consent.

SIGNED: Andrew Gent .... ON BEHALF OF: MR & MRS A. PLICANT .... DATE: 27th NOVEMBER '92'

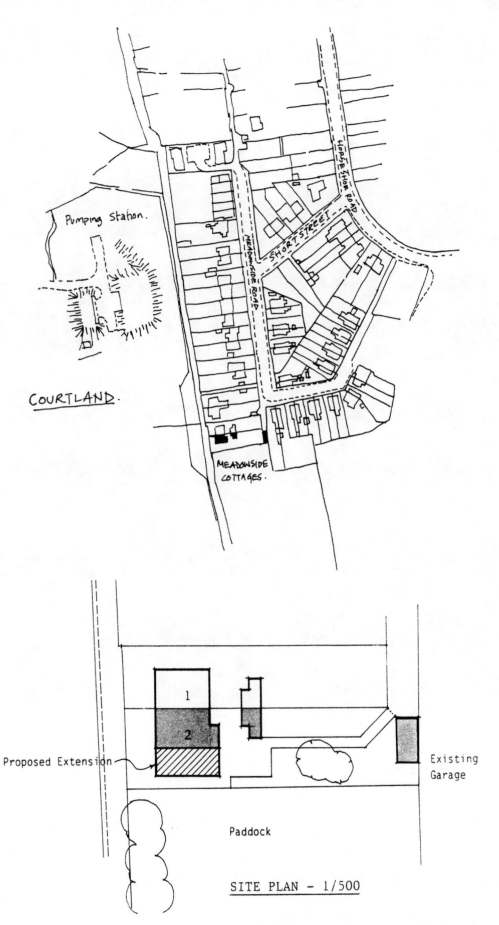

Pumping Station.

COURTLAND.

MEADOWSIDE ROAD

SHORT STREET

HORSE SHOE ROAD

MEADOWSIDE COTTAGES.

Proposed Extension

1

2

Existing Garage

Paddock

SITE PLAN - 1/500

drawing title		
LOCATION PLAN		
drawn by MWD	scale 1/2500, 1/500	
approved by	date 27 November 1991	
drawing number	9123/369-01	

PROPOSED WEST ELEVATION

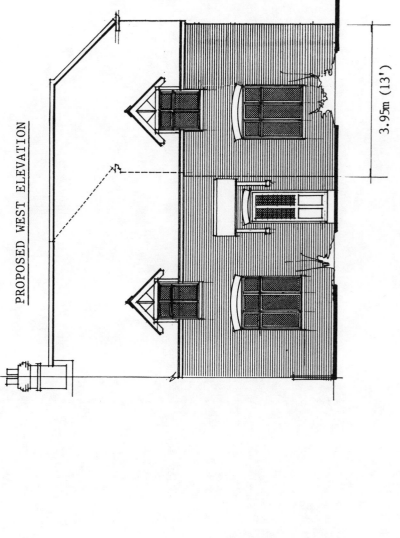

3.95m (13')

PROPOSED EAST ELEVATION

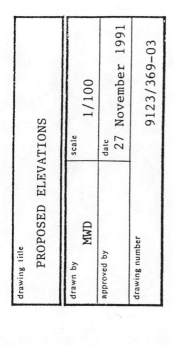

PROPOSED SOUTH ELEVATION

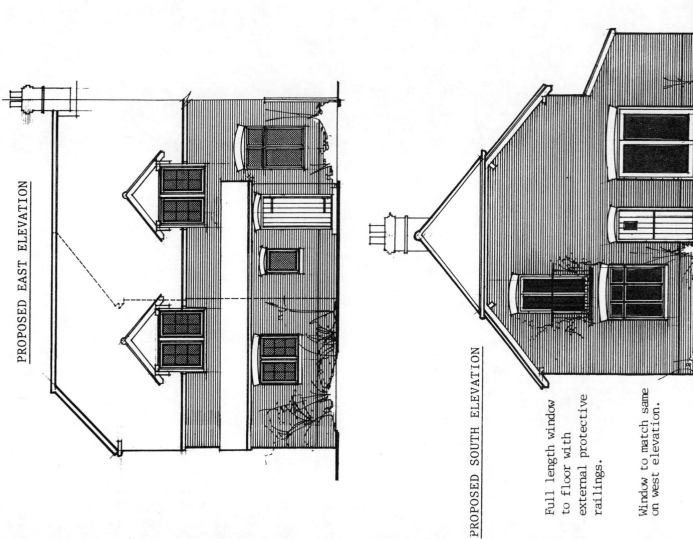

Full length window
to floor with
external protective
railings.

Window to match same
on west elevation.

drawing title		
PROPOSED ELEVATIONS		
drawn by	scale	1/100
MWD		
approved by	date	
	27 November 1991	
drawing number		
9123/369-03		

GROUND FLOOR PLANS

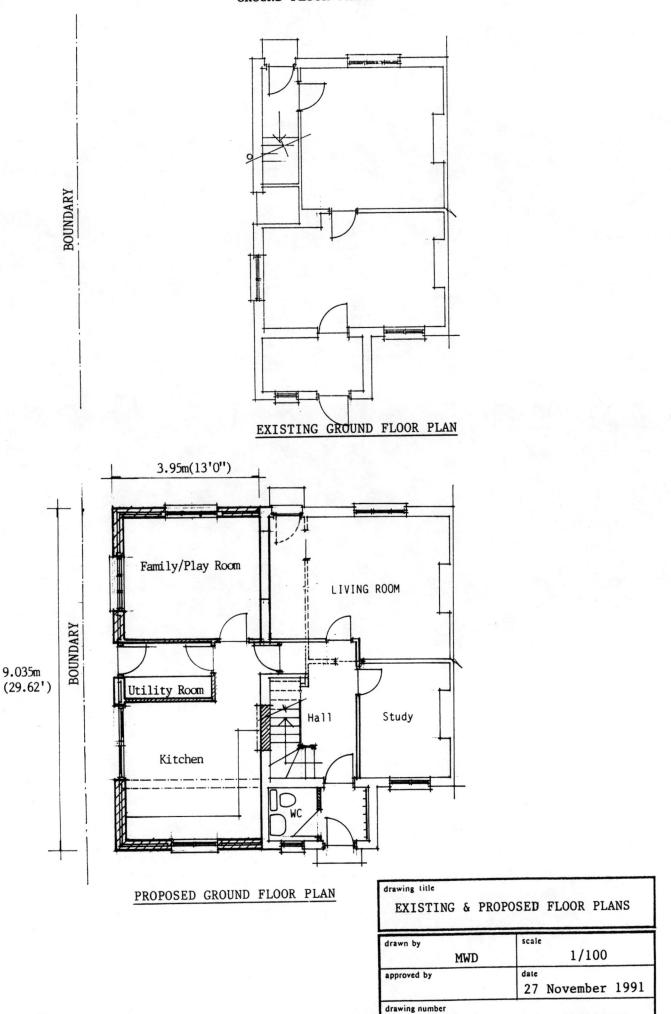

EXISTING GROUND FLOOR PLAN

3.95m(13'0")

BOUNDARY

9.035m
(29.62')

Family/Play Room

LIVING ROOM

Utility Room

Hall

Study

Kitchen

WC

PROPOSED GROUND FLOOR PLAN

drawing title		
EXISTING & PROPOSED FLOOR PLANS		
drawn by	scale	
MWD	1/100	
approved by	date	
	27 November 1991	
drawing number		
	9123/369-02	

FIRST FLOOR PLANS

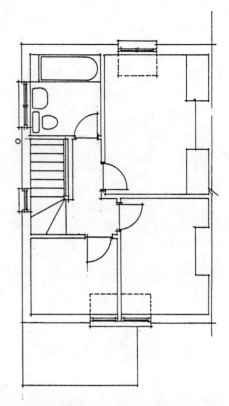

<u>EXISTING FIRST FLOOR PLAN</u>

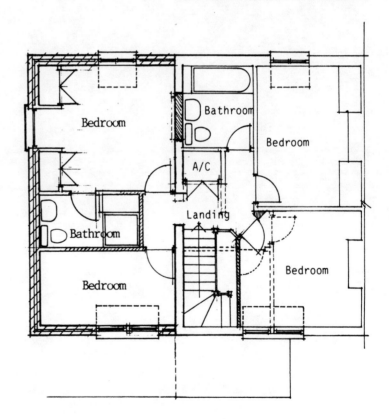

<u>PROPOSED FIRST FLOOR PLAN</u>

drawing title	
EXISTING & PROPOSED FLOOR PLANS	
drawn by MWD	**scale** 1/100
approved by	**date** 27 November 1991
drawing number	9123/369-02

CERTIFICATE A

UNDER SECTION 66 OF THE TOWN AND COUNTRY PLANNING ACT

I hereby certify that:

1. No person other than the applicant was an owner of any part of the land to which the application relates at the beginning of the period of 21 days before the date of the accompanying application.

2. None of the land to which the application relates constitutes or forms part of an agricultural holding.

   OR

   ~~The requisite Notice has been given to the following agricultural tenant(s):~~

Signed: *Andrew Gant* .... Date: 27ᵗʰ NOVEMBER '92'

on behalf of: MR & MRS A. PLICANT ....

CERTIFICATE B

UNDER SECTION 66 OF THE TOWN AND COUNTRY PLANNING ACT

I hereby certify that:

1. The requisite Notice No. 1 has been given to the owner(s) of the land to which the application relates.

   Name and address of owner: ....

   ....

   Date of Service of Notice No. 1: ....

2. None of the land to which the application relates constitutes or forms part of an agricultural holding.

   OR

   The requisite Notice has been given to the following agricutlural tenant(s):

Signed: .... Date: ....

on behalf of: ....

NOTICE NO.1

UNDER SECTION 66 OF THE TOWN AND COUNTRY PLANNING ACT

An application for planning permission is being made to Courtland District Council and you are owner/part owner of the application site.

Address of application site: ....

....

Description of proposal: ....

Name and address of applicant: ....

....

If you wish to make representations on this proposal, please do so within three weeks of receiving this notice to the Director of Development Services, Courtland District Council, Council Offices, Court Street, Courtland, Berks.

Signed: .... Date: ....

on behalf of: ....

UNDER SECTION 66 OF THE TOWN AND COUNTRY PLANNING ACT

I hereby certify that:

1. No person other than the applicant was owner of any part of the land to which the application relates at the beginning of the period of 21 days before the date of the accompanying application.

OR

2. Notice of the land to which the application relates as set out below has been given to the owners of an agricultural holding.

Signed .... Date ....

on behalf of ....

UNDER SECTION 65 OF THE TOWN AND COUNTRY PLANNING ACT

I hereby certify that:

1. The requisite Notice No. 1 has been given to the owner(s) of the land to which the application relates.

Name and address of owner ....

2. Date of Service of Notice No. 1 ....

3. None of the land to which the application relates comprises or forms part of an agricultural holding.

OR

The requisite Notice has been given to the following agricultural tenant(s).

Signed .... Date ....

on behalf of ....

UNDER SECTION 66 OF THE TOWN AND COUNTRY PLANNING ACT

An application for planning permission is being made to Council and you are owner/part owner of the application site.

Address of application site ....

Description of proposal ....

Name and address of applicant ....

If you wish to make representations to this proposal, please do so within three weeks of receiving this notice to the Director of Development Services, Council.

Signed .... Date ....

on behalf of ....

COURTLAND DISTRICT COUNCIL
HOUSEHOLDER PLANNING APPLICATION
APPLICATION FOR PERMISSION TO CARRY OUT DEVELOPMENT - TOWN AND COUNTRY PLANNING ACTS. THIS FORM IS ONLY TO BE USED FOR APPLICATIONS FOR EXTENSIONS TO HOUSES AND OTHER DEVELOPMENT WITHIN THE CURTILAGE OF SINGLE RESIDENTIAL DWELLINGS.

Please answer ALL QUESTIONS in BLOCK LETTERS. If a question is not applicable, answer N/A in space. Please send FOUR copies of this form and plans to:

FOR OFFICE USE ONLY

THE DIRECTOR OF PLANNING SERVICES,
COURTLAND DISTRICT COUNCIL,
COUNCIL OFFICES, COURT STREET,
COURTLAND, BERKSHIRE

1.		APPLICANT'S NAME	MR & MRS. A. N. OTHER
		ADDRESS	20 THE MOORS COURTLAND
		POSTCODE	CT5 6KD PHONE (0441) 63901
2.	If the applicant has an agent, all correspondence will be sent to the agent.	AGENT'S NAME ADDRESS	N/A.
		CONTACT NAME	N/A. PHONE
3.	Show the site outline in RED on the plans	SITE ADDRESS OR LOCATION	20 THE MOORS, COURTLAND. CT5 6KD
4.	WHAT IS THE APPLICATION FOR? Give brief details, including whether proposal is for single storey or two storey construction.	PROPOSAL	TWO STOREY SIDE AND REAR EXTENSION. SINGLE STOREY REAR EXTENSION AND ALTERATIONS TO EXISTING VEHICULAR ACCESS
5.	LIST ALL PLANS AND DRAWINGS SUBMITTED WITH THIS APPLICATION		LOCATION PLAN 1:2500, SITE PLAN 1:500 FLOOR PLANS 1:100, ELEVATIONS 1:100
6.	WILL THE PROPOSED EXTERNAL MATERIALS (WALLS AND ROOF) MATCH THE EXISTING?	YES/NO	If no, give details of materials to be used.
7.	IS THE SITE BOUNDARY TO BE ALTERED?	YES/NO	If yes, give details on the plans.
8.	(a) WILL SURFACE WATER DRAINAGE BE ALTERED?	YES/NO	If yes, give details on the plans.
	(b) WILL FOUL WATER DRAINAGE BE ALTERED?	YES/NO	If yes, give details on the plans.
9.	ARE ANY TREES TO BE FELLED?	YES/NO	If yes, give details on the plans.
10.	WILL ANY PEDESTRIAN OR VEHICULAR ACCESS BE ALTERED?	YES/NO	If yes, give details on the plans.
11.	IS FEE ENCLOSED?	YES/NO	If no, give reasons why.

I hereby apply for permission in respect of the particulars described above and in the attached plans and drawings. If planning permission is granted, the development must be carried out strictly in accordance with the approved plans. Failure to do so could result in enforcement action being taken. Permission under the Town & Country Planning Acts does not obviate the possible need to apply for Building Regulations Approval or any other necessary Consent.

SIGNED: _A.N. Other_   ON BEHALF OF: _SELF_   DATE: _15.04.92_

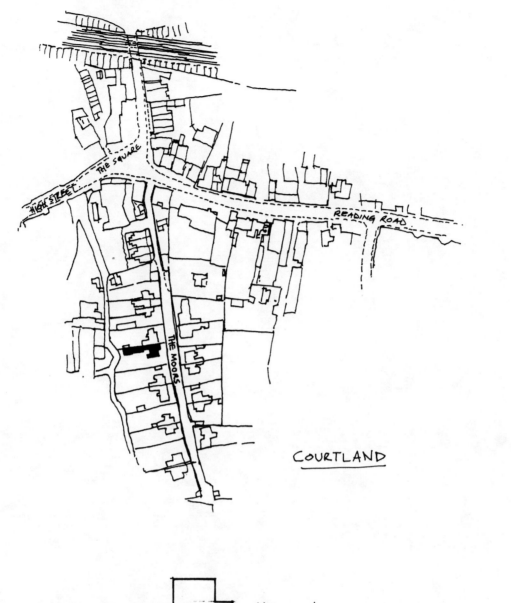

COURTLAND

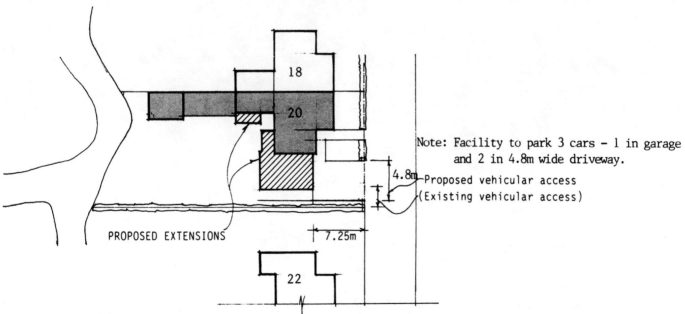

Note: Facility to park 3 cars – 1 in garage
and 2 in 4.8m wide driveway.

4.8m Proposed vehicular access
(Existing vehicular access)

PROPOSED EXTENSIONS

7.25m

18

20

22

SITE PLAN – 1/500

drawing title	
LOCATION & SITE PLANS	
drawn by	scale
MWD	1/2500,1/500
approved by	date
	9 April 1992
drawing number	
	9208/387–03

PROPOSED EAST ELEVATION

PROPOSED WEST ELEVATION

drawing title		
PROPOSED ELEVATIONS		
drawn by MWD	scale	1/100
approved by	date	
	15 April 1992	
drawing number	9208/387-05	

PROPOSED SOUTH ELEVATION

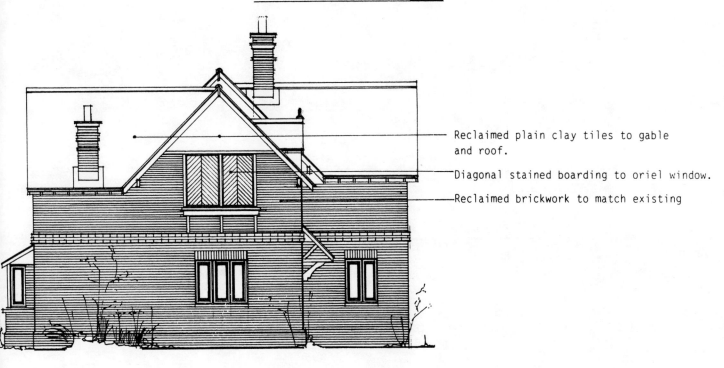

Reclaimed plain clay tiles to gable and roof.

Diagonal stained boarding to oriel window.

Reclaimed brickwork to match existing

drawing title		
PROPOSED ELEVATIONS		
drawn by MWD	scale 1/100	
approved by	date 15 April 1992	
drawing number	9208/387-05	

PROPOSED GROUND FLOOR PLAN

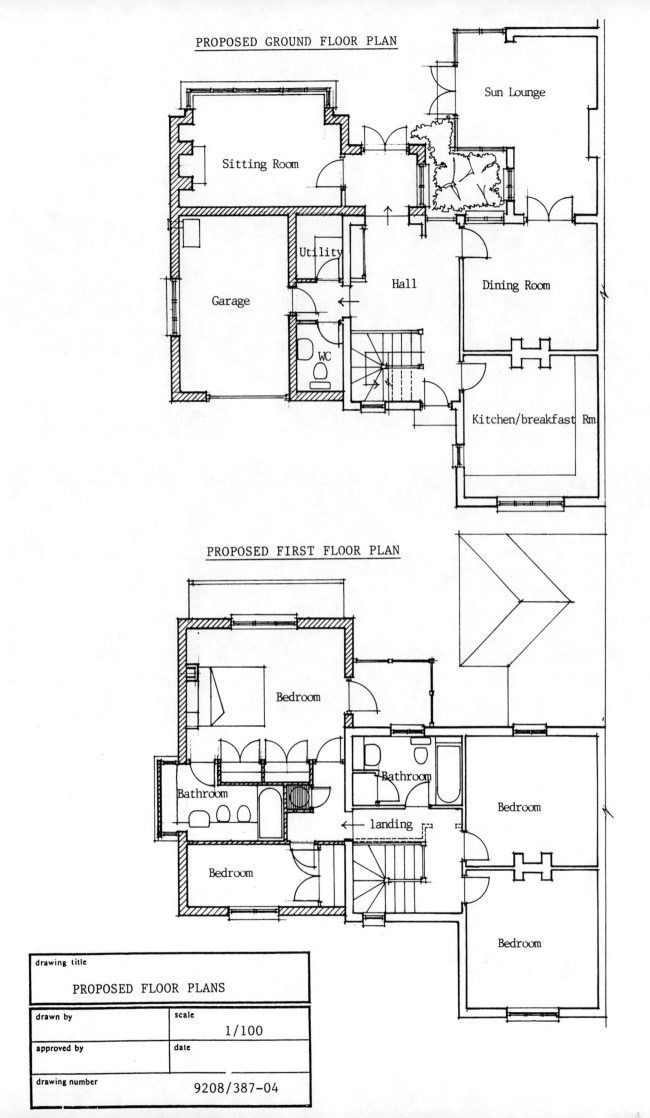

Sitting Room

Sun Lounge

Utility

Hall

Dining Room

Garage

WC

Kitchen/breakfast Rm.

PROPOSED FIRST FLOOR PLAN

Bedroom

Bathroom

Bathroom

Bedroom

landing

Bedroom

Bedroom

drawing title		
PROPOSED FLOOR PLANS		
drawn by	scale	
	1/100	
approved by	date	
drawing number	9208/387-04	

CERTIFICATE A

UNDER SECTION 66 OF THE TOWN AND COUNTRY PLANNING ACT

I hereby certify that:

1. No person other than the applicant was an owner of any part of the land to which the application relates at the beginning of the period of 21 days before the date of the accompanying application.

2. None of the land to which the application relates constitutes or forms part of an agricultural holding.

    OR

    ~~The requisite Notice has been given to the following agricultural tenant(s):~~

Signed: ....*Alan Ther*........................... Date: ......15.04.92..................

on behalf of: ....SELF...

CERTIFICATE B

UNDER SECTION 66 OF THE TOWN AND COUNTRY PLANNING ACT

I hereby certify that:

1. The requisite Notice No. 1 has been given to the owner(s) of the land to which the application relates.

    Name and address of owner: ....

    ....

    Date of Service of Notice No. 1: ....

2. None of the land to which the application relates constitutes or forms part of an agricultural holding.

    OR

    The requisite Notice has been given to the following agricutlural tenant(s):

Signed: .... Date: ....

on behalf of: ....

NOTICE NO.1

UNDER SECTION 66 OF THE TOWN AND COUNTRY PLANNING ACT

An application for planning permission is being made to Courtland District Council and you are owner/part owner of the application site.

Address of application site: ....

....

Description of proposal: ....

Name and address of applicant: ....

....

If you wish to make representations on this proposal, please do so within three weeks of receiving this notice to the Director of Development Services, Courtland District Council, Council Offices, Court Street, Courtland, Berks.

Signed: .... Date: ....

on behalf of: ....

GLOSSARY

GLOSSARY

GLOSSARY

Amenity: A word much loved by planners, an all embracing description of virtually anything that is beneficial or desirable in terms of the physical or visual environment. It is often used in reasons for the refusal of an application so that the arguments used can be as wide ranging as possible.

Amenity Space: If prefixed by 'private' this usually means back garden area. If prefixed by 'public' it can refer to areas of public open space such as verges or recreation grounds or commons.

Area of Outstanding Natural Beauty: See page 35.

Building Line: See page 42.

Circular Advice: This refers to a series of guidance documents issued by the Government to express its policies towards various planning matters, or to explain its intentions with regard to recent legislation.

Condition: See page 30.

Conservation Area: See page 35.

Curtilage: A parcel of land which includes a building may be described as the 'curtilage' of that building. In the case of domestic planning applications it simply refers to the land which belongs to the house, the extent of the 'curtilage' being defined by the boundaries of the garden. The legal definition can sometimes be important, if for instance, the 'curtilage' of a house has been extended to include agricultural land without first obtaining planning permission.

Development Plan: This is a general term used to denote the most relevant statutory Local, District, City or Borough (etc) Plan for any particular area. See page 73.

Enforcement Notice: See page 82.

Four Year Rule: See page 80.

General Development Order: This is a piece of planning legislation issued by the Government which sets out the way planning applications should be dealt with and the procedures to be followed by Planning Authorities. It also stipulates what development does not require planning permission. The GDO is periodically updated and amended.

Green Belt: See page 35.

Informal Hearing: See page 70

Listed Building: This is a building which has been 'listed' by the Department of the Environment due to its special historic or architectural interest. Its 'listed' status creates a wide range of very serious responsibilities and restrictions upon the owner. Doing any unauthorised work to a Listed Building is a criminal offence.

GLOSSARY

Listed Building Consent: This is applied for in much the same way as a Planning Application. It is required for any works to a Listed Building, either internal or external, which are not strictly a repair using traditional methods and the same materials. Failure to apply for Listed Building Consent can result in an unlimited fine and up to two years in prison.

Local Plan: See page 73.

MRTPI: Member of the Royal Town Planning Institute. This is achieved by most fully qualified and experienced planners.

National Park: See page 35.

Permitted Development: Those developments described in the GDO which do not require planning permission.

Planning Contravention Notice: See page 81.

Planning Policy Guidance: This refers to a series of Guidance Notes issued by the Government to indicate what planning policies the Government itself supports. PPG's are read closely by Local Authority Planning Departments, Applicants and those involved in Planning Appeals - including the Inspector. The most relevant to householder planning applications is PPG1 entitled 'General Policy and Principles'.

Primary Window/Secondary Window: These phrases are sometimes used by planners to distinguish between windows which will be considered relevant in terms of overlooking and those that will not. A primary window would be a window to a habitable room such as a bedroom or kitchen or sitting room. A secondary window would be to a non-habitable room such as a bathroom, the staircase, landing or utility room.

Public Inquiry: See page 71.

Requisition for Information Notice: See page 81.

Structure Plan: See page 73.

Ten Year Rule: See page 80.

Tree Preservation Order: See page 85.

Use Classes Order: This is a piece of planning legislation issued by the Government to categorise the vast range of possible uses of land or buildings. It specifies a series of separate "Use Classes" into which most activities will fit. It also specifies when planning permission is required to change from one 'use' to another. For example, the use of a building as a private house (whether it was built as one or not) is called a C3 use. To change from a C3 use to a B1 use (offices and light industrial) would require planning permission. To change from an A3 (restaurant/takeaway) use to an A1 (shop) use would not normally require permission. Those uses which are considered too unique to fit within any particular category are called 'sui-generis' uses. An example is car sales.

Written Representations: See page 70.